Contents

W9-AZA-520

Contents

Punchouts

Name _____

Strategy Workshop

As you listen to the story "The Sandwich," by Stephen Krensky, you will stop from time to time to do some activities on these practice pages. These activities will help you think about different strategies that can help you read better. After completing each activity, you will discuss what you've written with your classmates and talk about how to use these strategies.

Remember, strategies can help you become a better reader. Good readers

- use strategies whenever they read

- use different strategies before, during, and after reading

- think about how strategies will help them

Copyright © Houghton Mifflin Company. All rights reserved.

Name _____

Strategy 1: Predict/Infer

Use this strategy before and during reading to help make predictions about what happens next or what you're going to learn.

Here's how to use the Predict/Infer Strategy:

1. Think about the title, the illustrations, and what you have read so far.

2. Tell what you think will happen next—or what you will learn. Thinking about what you already know about the subject may help.

3. Try to figure out things the author does not say directly.

Listen as your teacher begins "The Sandwich." When your teacher stops, complete the activity with a partner.

What do you think might happen in the story?

_____

_____

As you listen to the story, you might want to change your prediction or write a new one here.

_____

_____

Copyright © Houghton Mifflin Company. All rights reserved.

Name _____

Strategy 2: Phonics/Decoding

Use this strategy during reading when you come across a word you don't know.

Here's how to use the Phonics/Decoding Strategy:

1. Look carefully at the word.
2. Look for word parts that you know and think about the sounds for the letters.
3. Blend the sounds to read the word.
4. Ask yourself if this is a word you know. Does it make sense in the sentence?
5. If not, ask yourself if there's anything else you can try. Should I look in the dictionary?

Listen to your teacher read. When your teacher stops, use the Phonics/Decoding Strategy.

Now write down the steps you used to decode the word *powder*.

_____

_____

_____

_____

Copyright © Houghton Mifflin Company. All rights reserved.

Name _____

Strategy 3: Monitor/Clarify

Use this strategy during reading whenever you're confused about what you are reading.

Here's how to use the Monitor/Clarify Strategy:

- Ask yourself if what you're reading makes sense—or if you are learning what you need to learn.
- If you don't understand something, reread, look at the illustrations, or read ahead.

Listen to your teacher read. When your teacher stops, answer the questions with a partner.

1. What is Lionel's problem?

_____

_____

2. Can you tell from listening to the story what Lionel's problem is? Why or why not?

_____

_____

3. How can you find out what Lionel's problem is if you're confused?

_____

_____

Copyright © Houghton Mifflin Company. All rights reserved.

Name _____

Strategy 4: Question

Use this strategy during and after reading to ask questions about important ideas in the story.

Here's how to use the Question Strategy:

- Ask yourself questions about important ideas in the story.
- Ask yourself if you can answer these questions.
- If you can't answer the questions, reread and look for answers in the text. Thinking about what you already know and what you've read in the story may help you.

Listen to your teacher read. Then complete the activity with a partner to ask yourself questions about important ideas in the story.

Think about the story and respond below.

Write a question you might ask yourself at this point in the story.

_____

_____

_____

_____

Copyright © Houghton Mifflin Company. All rights reserved.

Name _____

Strategy 5: Evaluate

Use this strategy during and after reading to help you form an opinion about what you read.

Here's how to use the Evaluate Strategy:

- Think about how the author makes the story come alive and makes you want to read it.
- Think about what was entertaining, informative, or useful about the selection.
- Think about how well you understood the selection and whether you enjoyed reading it.

Listen to your teacher read. When your teacher stops, answer the questions with a partner.

1. Do you think this story is entertaining? Why?

   _____

   _____

2. Is the writing clear and easy to understand?

   _____

   _____

3. Did the author make the characters interesting and believable?

   _____

Copyright © Houghton Mifflin Company. All rights reserved.

Name _____

Strategy 6: Summarize

Use this strategy after reading to summarize what you read.

Here's how to use the Summarize Strategy:

- Think about the characters.
- Think about where the story takes place.
- Think about the problem in the story and how the characters solve it.
- Think about what happens in the beginning, middle, and end of the story.

Think about the story you just listened to. Answer the questions with a partner to show that you understand how to identify story parts that will help you summarize the story.

1. Who is the main character?

_____

2. Where does the story take place?

_____

3. What is the problem and how is it resolved?

_____

_____

Copyright © Houghton Mifflin Company. All rights reserved.

Name _____

The Sandwich, by Stephen Krensky

Lionel liked peanut butter and jelly sandwiches.
He didn't like jelly and peanut butter sandwiches.

Make a shopping list for your favorite lunch food.

My Lunch List

What is your favorite lunch? Draw a picture of
your lunch in the tray.

Copyright © Houghton Mifflin Company. All rights reserved.

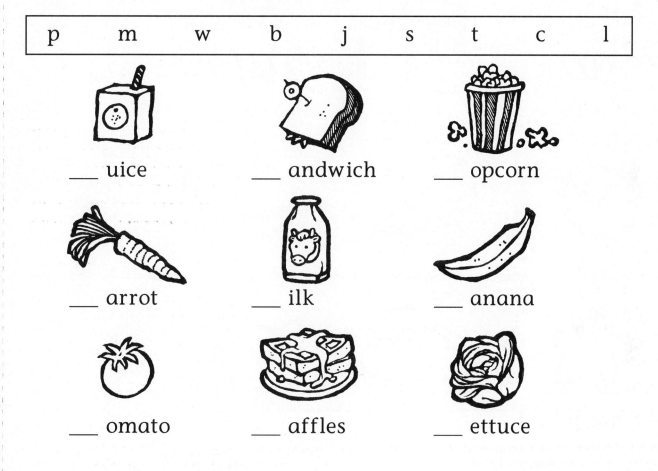

Name _____

Choose the letter that completes the name of each food. Write the letter on the line at the beginning of each word.

| p | m | w | b | j | s | t | c | l |

___ uice

___ andwich

___ opcorn

___ arrot

___ ilk

___ anana

___ omato

___ affles

___ ettuce

Writing Words You Know

Write a word you know on the line beside each beginning sound.

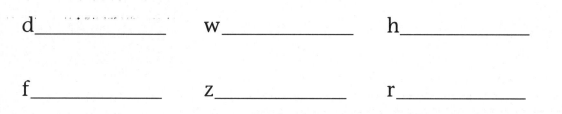

d_____   w_____   h_____

f_____   z_____   r_____

Copyright © Houghton Mifflin Company. All rights reserved.

Name _____

Circle the letter that stands for the sound you hear at the **end** of each picture name.

d t p

n d l

g p j

r l t

k s d

n b z

l r s

c t b

z m g

Writing Words You Know

Write a word you know on the line beside each ending sound.

_____p   _____l   _____n

_____t   _____b   _____m

Copyright © Houghton Mifflin Company. All rights reserved.

Name _____

Look at the pictures. Read the words in the box.
Write the word that names each picture.

stick	truck	drink
flag	clown	smile

_____   _____   _____

_____   _____   _____

Writing Words You Know

Write a word you know on the line beside each
beginning cluster.

br_____   fl_____   st_____

pr_____   gl_____   tr_____

Copyright © Houghton Mifflin Company. All rights reserved.

Name _____

Write the letters that stand for the beginning
sounds you hear in each picture name.

| br | fl | cl | tr | sn | cr | st |

Writing Words You Know

Write a word you know on the line beside
each cluster.

bl_____   fr_____   pl_____

dr_____   st_____   gl_____

Copyright © Houghton Mifflin Company. All rights reserved.

Name _____

Write **ch**, **sh**, **th**, or **wh** to finish each picture name.

tee_____   sandwi_____   _____ip

_____eat   bea_____   _____irty

_____ick   di_____   clo_____

_____

Writing Words You Know

Write a word you know on the line beside each beginning digraph.

sh_____   ch_____

wh_____   th_____

Copyright © Houghton Mifflin Company. All rights reserved.

Name _____

Write **ch**, **sh**, or **th** to complete each picture name. Then draw a line to connect the row of three pictures with the same sound.

pea_____   bu_____   _____umb

_____eep   _____air   pa_____

fi_____   _____orn   _____ain

Writing Words You Know

Write a word you know on the line beside each digraph.

_____ ch   _____ sh   _____ th

Copyright © Houghton Mifflin Company. All rights reserved.

Name _____

Complete each puzzle with the correct vowel. Then use the words to complete the sentences under each picture.

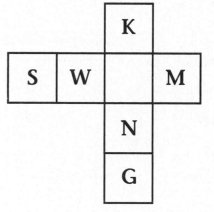

The _____ can
_____ very fast.

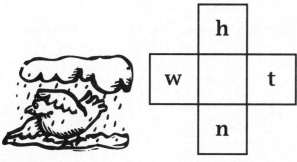

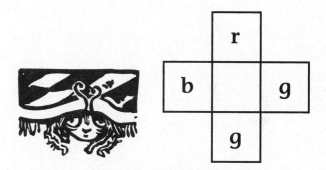

The _____ got
very _____.

The _____ hid under
the _____.

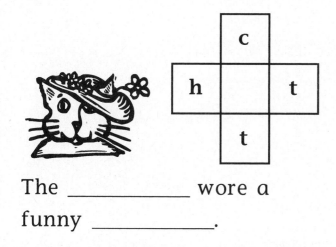

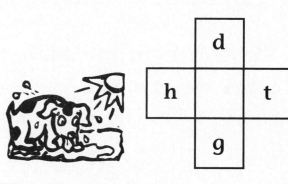

The _____ wore a
funny _____.

The sun made the
_____ very _____.

Copyright © Houghton Mifflin Company. All rights reserved.

Name _____

Write a letter on a line to build a word that has the same short vowel sound as the picture name.

____ an
____ ab
____ at

____ ot
____ od
____ op

____ ug
____ up
____ un

____ et
____ en
____ eg

____ ish
____ ist
____ ift

Writing Words You Know

Write a word you know on the line beside the short vowel sound. The word can have the vowel sound in it or begin with the short vowel sound.

a_____   e_____   i_____

o_____   u_____

Copyright © Houghton Mifflin Company. All rights reserved.

Name _____

Look at the pictures. Read the words in the box.
Write the word that names each picture.

bee	flute	leaf
gate	goat	tie
vine	nail	rope

_____   _____   _____

_____   _____   _____

_____   _____   _____

Writing Words You Know

Write a word you know on the lines with the
long vowel sound.

____ o ____ e   ____ a ____ e   ____ i ____ e

____ ee ____   ____ o ____ e

Copyright © Houghton Mifflin Company. All rights reserved.

Name _____

Add an *e* to the end of each group of letters.
Then draw a picture of the word you made.

can _____ [   ]

kit _____ [   ]

rop _____ [   ]

cub _____ [   ]

tre _____ [   ]

Writing Words You Know

Write a word you know with the long vowel
sound beside each vowel. The word can begin
with the vowel or have the vowel in it.

a_____   e_____   i_____

o_____   u_____

Copyright © Houghton Mifflin Company. All rights reserved.

Name _____

Silly Stories

Write your own silly story. Think of a silly character, such as a plant or animal that speaks, then fill in the blanks to complete the story.

One day, _____

came into our classroom. It _____

and then it _____ .

Finally, my teacher _____ .

Now write three sentences that tell more about what happened. Then draw your silly character in the box.

_____

_____

_____

_____

Copyright © Houghton Mifflin Company. All rights reserved.

Name _____

Silly Stories

Fill in the chart as you read the stories.

	Where do the silly stories in this theme take place?	What silly things do some of the characters do?
Dragon Gets By		
Julius		
Mrs. Brown Went to Town		

Copyright © Houghton Mifflin Company. All rights reserved.

Name _____

Making Words

When you put these letters together, they make words.

m + a + p = map  p + i + n = pin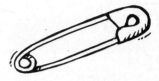

**Put these letters together to write words with
the short *a* and short *i* sound.**

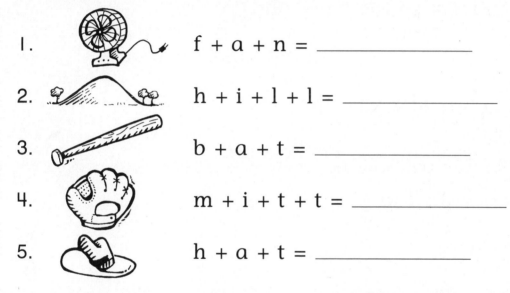

1. f + a + n = _____

2. h + i + l + l = _____

3. b + a + t = _____

4. m + i + t + t = _____

5. h + a + t = _____

**Now use the short *a* and short *i* words you wrote
above to complete the sentences below.**

6. The dog ran up the _____ .

7. Martin caught the ball in his _____ .

8. Juan turns on the _____ when he is hot.

9. I wear my _____ on my head.

10. Sue hit the ball with the _____ .

Copyright © Houghton Mifflin Company. All rights reserved.

Name _____

Shopping for Food

Write the correct word to finish each sentence.

Word Bank

bought	kitchen	roll	front	until

1. Mr. Janson went to the store and

   _____ many kinds of food.

2. He stood in line and paid for his food at the

   _____ of the store.

3. Mr. Janson waited in line _____

   it was his turn.

4. He did not let his cart _____

   away.

5. When he got home, he took the food into the

   _____.

**Write a sentence that tells about something that
you have bought.**

_____

_____

Copyright © Houghton Mifflin Company. All rights reserved.

Name _____

Words That Fit

Use words from the box to complete the sentences in the puzzle.

Word Bank

hungry vegetables shopping shoppers dairy balanced

Across

1. If you are buying food at a food store, you are _____ .

2. Carrots, peas, and spinach are _____ .

3. Milk, cheese, and ice cream are _____ products.

5. People who buy food at a food store are called _____ .

Down

4. When you need to eat, you feel _____ .

6. If you eat foods from the basic food groups, you have a _____ diet.

Copyright © Houghton Mifflin Company. All rights reserved.

Name _____

Story Map

**As you read the story, complete the story
map below.**

Who (Who is in the story?)

_____

Where (Where does the story take place?)

_____

_____

Beginning (pages 19–22) (What happens?)

_____

_____

Middle (pages 23–32) (What happens?)

_____

_____

End (pages 33–34) (What happens?)

_____

_____

Copyright © Houghton Mifflin Company. All rights reserved.

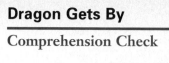

Name _____

Ask Away

Below are questions about the story *Dragon Gets By*.
Write an answer to each question.

1. Why didn't the food that Dragon
   bought at the store fit in his car?

   _____

2. What did Dragon plan to do so he could
   fit the food in his car?

   _____

   _____

3. Why couldn't Dragon fit in his car?

   _____

   _____

4. How did Dragon get his car home?

   _____

5. How did Dragon feel when he got home?

   _____

Copyright © Houghton Mifflin Company. All rights reserved.

Name _____

Story Structure

**Read the story and then answer the
questions on the next page.**

Raccoon's Party

Raccoon wanted someone to talk to,
but he lived alone. He decided to have
a party. He put up balloons and made
some good food. He invited a few friends
to come to his party. Soon his friends were
ringing the doorbell. Raccoon asked them
into his house. He enjoyed talking to his
friends. It wasn't long before they didn't have
anything else to say to each other. It was too
early for the party to end, so Raccoon invited
more friends to his party.

Lots of Raccoon's friends came to his party.
Everyone was having a great time. That is,
everyone except Raccoon. The house was so
crowded, Raccoon could barely move. The
party was so noisy that Raccoon couldn't
talk to any of his friends. Raccoon knew what
to do. He wiggled his way past everyone to
the front door and stepped out of his house.
He was glad to be outside where he could
finally get some peace and quiet!

Copyright © Houghton Mifflin Company. All rights reserved.

Name _____

Story Structure continued

**After you've read the story, answer
each question below.**

Who (Who is in the story?)

1. _____

2. _____

Where (Where does the story take place?)

3. _____

Beginning (What happens?)

4. _____

5. _____

Middle (What happens?)

6. _____

7. _____

8. _____

9. _____

End (What happens?)

10. _____

Copyright © Houghton Mifflin Company. All rights reserved.

Shopping for Endings

Example:

help + s

helps

help + ed

helped

help + ing

helping

Look at each base word and ending. Put each base word together with an ending to make a new word. Write the new word on the line. Then read the new word.

1. work   + s   + ed

    _____   _____

2. play   + s   , + ed

    _____   _____

3. talk   + ed   + ing

    _____   _____

4. eat   + s   + ing

    _____   _____

5. stay   + s   + ing

    _____   _____

Copyright © Houghton Mifflin Company. All rights reserved.

Name _____

Apple or Fish?

► Five Spelling Words have the short **a** vowel sound that you hear at the beginning of .

► Five Spelling Words have the short **i** vowel sound that you hear in .

► The words **was** and **I** are special.

Write the Spelling Words with the short *a* vowel sound under the apple and the short *i* vowel sound under the fish.

apple

fish

_____   _____

_____   _____

_____   _____

_____   _____

_____   _____

Write the two Spelling Words that do not have the vowel sounds you hear in *apple* or *fish*.

_____   _____

Spelling Words

1. bag
2. win
3. is
4. am
5. his
6. has
7. ran
8. if
9. dig
10. sat
11. was*
12. I*

Copyright © Houghton Mifflin Company. All rights reserved.

Name _____

Spelling Spree

Word Clues Write a Spelling Word that answers each clue.

1. Something to carry things in _____

2. Something you do with a shovel

   _____

3. A word that can be found in **ham**, **jam**,

   Pam, and **Sam** _____

4. This word has only one letter

   _____

5. Add **h** to the beginning of **as** to

   make this word _____

6. Add **w** to the beginning of **as** to

   make this word _____

7. The word **is** can be found inside

   this word _____

8. A word that rhymes with **cat** and

   rat _____

Spelling Words

1. bag
2. win
3. is
4. am
5. his
6. has
7. ran
8. if
9. dig
10. sat
11. was*
12. I*

Copyright © Houghton Mifflin Company. All rights reserved.

Name _____

Proofreading and Writing

Proofreading **In the letter below, find and circle**
four Spelling Words that are not spelled correctly.
Write each word correctly.

Copyright © Houghton Mifflin Company. All rights reserved.

Dear Chris,

I play on a baseball team. Our team name

iz the Dragons. My hat has a picture of a

dragon on it! I play third base. Iff we win our

next two games, we will be in first place. I sat

out today's game. My knee wus hurting. I hope I

can play next week, and I hope the Dragons wen!

Your friend,

Bob

1. _____		3. _____	
2. _____		4. _____	

Spelling Words

1. bag
2. win
3. is
4. am
5. his
6. has
7. ran
8. if
9. dig
10. sat
11. was*
12. I*

Write a Letter **Write a letter to one of your**
friends. Tell about something that has happened
to you. Write your letter on another sheet of
paper. Use Spelling Words from the list.

Name _____

Pairs of Pears

Draw a line from each word on the left to a word on the right that sounds the same but has a different meaning.

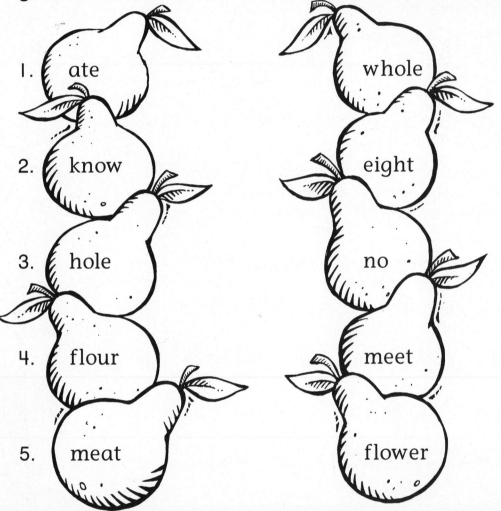

1. ate
2. know
3. hole
4. flour
5. meat

whole
eight
no
meet
flower

Choose one of the pairs of words. Write two sentences.
Use one of the words in each sentence.

_____

_____

_____

Copyright © Houghton Mifflin Company. All rights reserved.

Lightning Sentences

▶ A sentence tells what someone or something does.
Write *yes* or *no* to tell whether each of these is a sentence.

1. Lightning struck the tree. _____

2. Rain splashes against the window. _____

3. A strong wind. _____

4. Dark clouds fill the sky. _____

5. We heard a loud clap of thunder. _____

6. We could see the lightning. _____

7. Shovels the snow off the sidewalk. _____

8. Snowflakes float to the ground. _____

9. Makes it warm outside. _____

10. The rain caused a flood. _____

Copyright © Houghton Mifflin Company. All rights reserved.

Name _____

Follow the Sentence Road

A sentence tells what someone or something does.
**Find the store by coloring only the pieces
of the road that are complete sentences.**

A large fly.

My dog runs fast.

The tiger is in the river.

Live in the ocean.

Pigs in the mud.

The rabbit hops away.

The snake.

The cat is by the fireplace.

STORE

OPEN

Five cows are in the field.

Reach with their necks.

Copyright © Houghton Mifflin Company. All rights reserved.

Name _____

Cans of Sentences

Circle the cans with complete sentences.

mom bought two cans of soup

places the cans in the cupboard

the peaches in this can are sweet

there are eight cans on the shelf

opened the can of peas

some kinds of juice are sold in cans

cans of green beans

the labels tell what is inside each can

Write each sentence you circled. Remember to use capital letters and periods.

1. _____

2. _____

3. _____

4. _____

5. _____

Copyright © Houghton Mifflin Company. All rights reserved.

Name _____

Who Is Dragon?

Read the questions in the circles. Write your answers in the boxes.

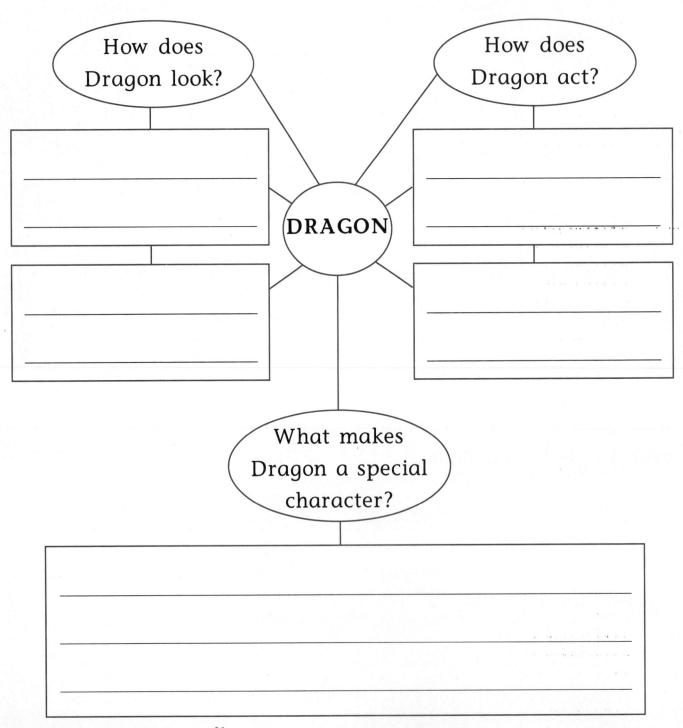

How does
Dragon look?

How does
Dragon act?

DRAGON

What makes
Dragon a special
character?

Copyright © Houghton Mifflin Company. All rights reserved.

Name _____

Telling More

Read each sentence. Rewrite the sentences so they tell more about the characters.

Example: David likes to write.

David likes to write long, silly stories.

1. Jessie has long hair.

_____

_____

2. The horse is wild.

_____

_____

3. The woman is strong.

_____

_____

4. The ape is silly.

_____

_____

5. My dog is a fast runner.

_____

_____

Copyright © Houghton Mifflin Company. All rights reserved.

Name _____

Revising Your Story

Put a check next to the sentences that tell about your story.

Superstar

☐ My story has a good beginning.

☐ My story has a middle.

☐ My story has a good ending.

☐ My story has a good title.

☐ I used complete sentences.

Rising Star

☐ My story needs a good beginning.

☐ The middle of my story could be better.

☐ My story needs an ending.

☐ I need to add a good title to my story.

☐ Some of my sentences aren't complete.

Copyright © Houghton Mifflin Company. All rights reserved.

Copyright © Houghton Mifflin Company. All rights reserved.

Name _____

Writing Sentences

**A Funny Clown Read each sentence. Write
the parts of the sentence on the lines.**

1. The clown ran around the ring.

   Who or What? _____

   What happened? _____

2. The clown jumped up and down.

   Who or What? _____

   What happened? _____

3. The little dog chased the clown.

   Who or What? _____

   What happened? _____

Write one or two sentences to finish the story.

_____

_____

_____

Name _____

Spelling Words

These Spelling Words are words that you use in your writing. Look carefully at how they are spelled. Write the missing letters in the Spelling Words below. Use the words in the box.

1. w____s

2. m____

3. s____d

4. th____

5. h____e

6. ____ny

7. th____

8. wi____

9. i____

10. a____

11. y____

12. o____

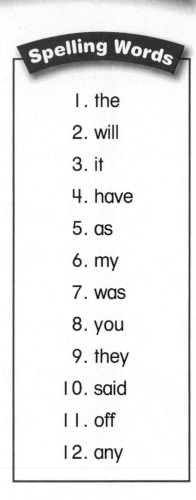

Spelling Words

1. the
2. will
3. it
4. have
5. as
6. my
7. was
8. you
9. they
10. said
11. off
12. any

Write the Spelling Words below.

_____ _____

_____ _____

_____ _____

_____ _____

_____ _____

_____ _____

Copyright © Houghton Mifflin Company. All rights reserved.

Name _____

Spelling Spree

Use the Spelling Words to complete the sentences. Write the words in the circus tent.

1. He ___ happy to go to the circus.
2. He wanted to see ___ clowns.
3. They ___ be funny.
4. Do ___ think the show will start on time?
5. "Yes, ___ will begin at six o'clock," said Tom.
6. Are there ___ elephants in the show?
7. "No, ___ are coming tomorrow."
8. We will ___ to come back to see them.

Copyright © Houghton Mifflin Company. All rights reserved.

Spelling Words

1. the
2. will
3. it
4. have
5. as
6. my
7. was
8. you
9. they
10. said
11. off
12. any

1. _____ 5. _____
2. _____ 6. _____
3. _____ 7. _____
4. _____ 8. _____

Write the Spelling Words that rhyme with *sky* and *jazz*.

9. _____   10. _____

Name _____

Proofreading and Writing

Proofreading Find and circle misspelled Spelling Words in this story. Then write each word correctly.

Spelling Words

1. the
2. will
3. it
4. have
5. as
6. my
7. was
8. you
9. they
10. said
11. off
12. any

    Holly wuz the Walls's funny little kitten. Thay liked to watch her get up on her hind legs and dance around. One day she hopped into an open bureau drawer and fell asleep.

    Brianna Wall came into the room. "I haf to get my new shorts," she sed. She opened the drawer and Holly jumped up. Brianna was surprised! Then the drawer fell. The clothes landed on the floor. Holly ran of!

1. _____ 2. _____ 3. _____

4. _____ 5. _____

Write Funny Sentences Write sentences about funny things or something that happens that is funny. Use as many Spelling Words as you can in your sentences.

Copyright © Houghton Mifflin Company. All rights reserved.

Julius

Phonics Skill Short Vowels
o, u, e; VCCV Pattern

Name _____

This Little Piggy

Write each word from the Word Bank under the pig that has the matching vowel sound.

Word Bank

hog	enjoy	mud	pigpen	grunt	hot

bed

box

cup

_____   _____   _____

_____   _____   _____

Finish the sentences below. Use the words from the Word Bank.

1. Pigs live in a _____ near the barn.

2. They make a sound like a _____ .

3. Sometimes pigs get _____ in the sun.

4. They lie in _____ to stay cool.

5. Pigs _____ the way it feels.

6. A pig can also be called a _____ .

Copyright © Houghton Mifflin Company. All rights reserved.

Name _____

Pick a Pet

Write a word from the box to complete each sentence.

Word Bank

| brought | reason | special | surprise |

1. One day Mom _____ home a kitten.

2. It was a big _____ to everyone in the family.

3. The _____ Mom got the kitten was that she wanted a pet.

4. She thought the kitten was _____ because it had blue eyes.

What kind of pet would you like to have? Draw a picture of it. Write a sentence to tell why it would be a special pet.

_____

_____

_____

Copyright © Houghton Mifflin Company. All rights reserved.

Mind Your Manners

Living with other people can be difficult. Here are some rules to help everyone get along. Use the vocabulary words to complete the sentences.

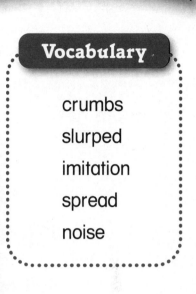

Vocabulary

crumbs

slurped

imitation

spread

noise

1. Use a broom to sweep up cookie

_____ on the floor.

2. Turn the radio low to keep the

_____ down.

3. Keep your toys in one place so they are

not _____ out.

4. After you have _____
a drink, say "Excuse me!"

5. If you act like an animal, do the

_____ outside.

Think about the rules at home. Write one of the rules on the lines.

_____

_____

Copyright © Houghton Mifflin Company. All rights reserved.

Theme 1: **Silly Stories**   27

Name _____

Fantasy and Realism Chart

Use the chart below to help you keep track of
things that could really happen and things that
could not.

Could Really Happen	Could Not Really Happen
_____	_____
_____	_____
_____	_____
_____	_____
_____	_____
_____	_____
_____	_____
_____	_____

Copyright © Houghton Mifflin Company. All rights reserved.

Name _____

Hidden Message

Use the clues to complete the puzzle.

1. Julius made big _____ .
2. Julius and Maya went to the store to try on _____ , hats, and shoes.
3. They loved to _____ to jazz records.
4. Julius loved to eat peanut butter from a _____ .
5. Mom and Dad said Julius made too much _____ .
6. Maya taught Julius good _____ .
7. Maya and Julius liked to _____ at the playground.

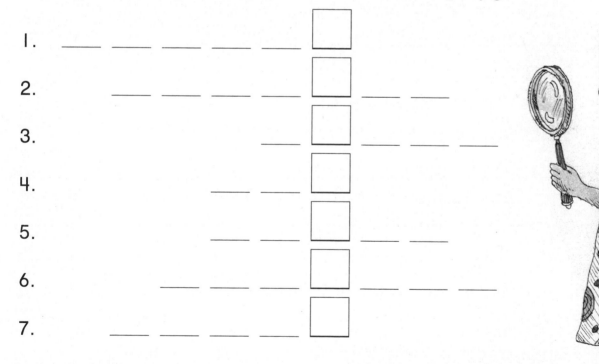

1. __ __ __ __ __ __ [ ]
2. __ __ __ __ __ [ ] __ __
3. __ __ __ [ ] __ __ __
4. __ __ [ ] __
5. __ __ __ __ [ ] __ __
6. __ __ __ [ ] __ __
7. __ __ __ __ [ ] __ __

Write the letters from the boxes to find out what Maya and Julius taught each other.

[ ] [ ] [ ] [ ] [ ] [ ] [ ]

Copyright © Houghton Mifflin Company. All rights reserved.

Name _____

Fantasy and Realism

**Read the story below and then answer the questions
on the next page.**

A Picnic in the Park

It was such a nice day, Gloria decided to go
to the park. She packed a picnic. Then she
called her dog, Ben.

"Let's go to the park, Ben. I packed a picnic for
us." Ben came running. He stopped in front of
Gloria. Ben gave her a big dog lick.

"I love the park," Ben said. "What did
you pack for me to eat?"

"I packed your favorite dog food and
some bones," answered Gloria.

"This is going to be a great day!" said Ben.
He put on his sunglasses. "I can hardly wait to go
down the slide. And I'll push you on the swing."

Ben ran to get some things he wanted to
take to the park. He got his swim fins and a
big towel. He got his best ball and a good
book to read.

"Ben, you don't need all that stuff!" Gloria
said. "Yes I do!" Ben answered.

"Okay, but you forgot the most important thing,"
Gloria said.

"My leash! I'll get it!" cried Ben.

Copyright © Houghton Mifflin Company. All rights reserved.

Name _____

Fantasy and Realism continued

Answer the questions. Use complete sentences.

1. Which character could be real?

   _____

2. Which character does make-believe things?

   _____

3. Name three things in the story that are make-believe.

   _____

   _____

   _____

   _____

4. Name three things in the story that are real.

   _____

   _____

   _____

What do you think Gloria and Ben will do at the park? On another sheet of paper, write an ending for the story.

Copyright © Houghton Mifflin Company. All rights reserved.

Name _____

Pet Show

**Mrs. Johnson's class had a show-and-tell about pets.
Read the rhymes to find out about the animals at the
show. Write words from the box to complete the rhymes.**

Word Bank

| ants | cat | rabbit | fish | pig |

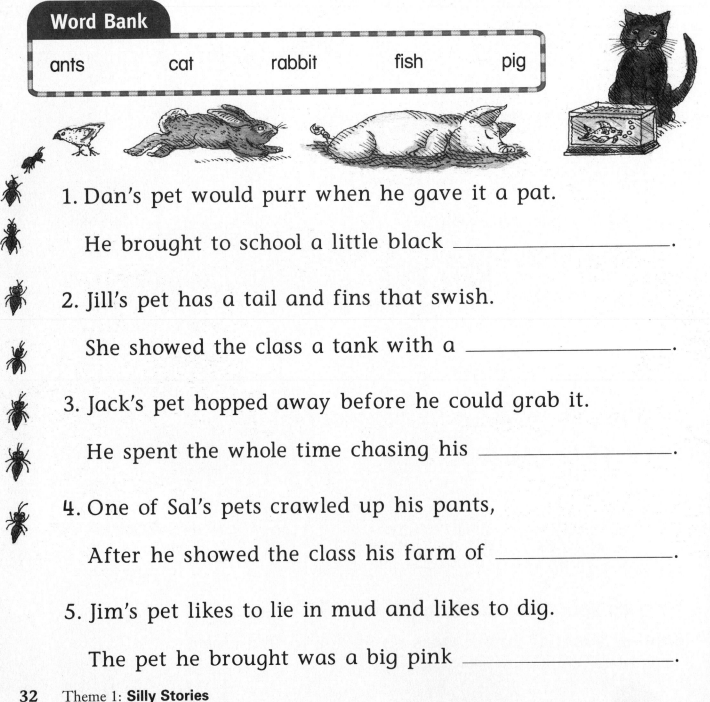

1. Dan's pet would purr when he gave it a pat.

   He brought to school a little black _____.

2. Jill's pet has a tail and fins that swish.

   She showed the class a tank with a _____.

3. Jack's pet hopped away before he could grab it.

   He spent the whole time chasing his _____.

4. One of Sal's pets crawled up his pants,

   After he showed the class his farm of _____.

5. Jim's pet likes to lie in mud and likes to dig.

   The pet he brought was a big pink _____.

Copyright © Houghton Mifflin Company. All rights reserved.

Name _____

What's the Sound?

► The vowel sound in **job** and **pop** is called the short **o** sound. The short **o** sound may be spelled **o**. The words **from** and **of** are special. The vowel **o** does not spell the short **o** sound.

► The vowel sound in **pet** and **leg** is called the short **e** sound. The word **any** is special. The short **e** sound is not spelled with the vowel **e**.

► The vowel sound in **nut** and **rug** is called the short **u** sound.

Spelling Words

1. fox
2. wet
3. nut
4. job
5. leg
6. fun
7. went
8. mop
9. hug
10. from*
11. any*
12. of *

Write each Spelling Word under the pet with the matching vowel sound.

short o   short u   short e

_____   _____   _____

_____   _____   _____

_____   _____   _____

Now write the 3 words with the * beside them.

_____   _____   _____

Copyright © Houghton Mifflin Company. All rights reserved.

Theme 1: **Silly Stories**   33

Name _____

Spelling Spree

Word Groups Think about the meaning of each group of words. Write the Spelling Word that goes with each group.

Spelling Words

1. fox
2. wet
3. nut
4. job
5. leg
6. fun
7. went
8. mop
9. hug
10. from*
11. any*
12. of*

1. broom, rake, _____

2. bear, wolf, _____

3. arm, foot, _____

4. all, some, _____

5. bean, grape, _____

6. work, office, _____

7. gone, left, _____

8. hold, squeeze, _____

Write a sentence using one of the Spelling Words that didn't go with any of the groups.

9. _____

_____

Copyright © Houghton Mifflin Company. All rights reserved.

Name _____

Proofreading and Writing

Proofreading Circle four Spelling Words that are wrong in this letter.

Dear Grandmother,

    I have a new dog. His name is Josh.

He is funn to play with. Josh likes to run

frm one side of the yard to the other.

Sometimes it is a big job to take care uf

Josh. He likes to sit in his water dish. He

gets all weet. Then he shakes himself.

        Love,

        Rita

Copyright © Houghton Mifflin Company. All rights reserved.

Spelling Words

1. fox
2. wet
3. nut
4. job
5. leg
6. fun
7. went
8. mop
9. hug
10. from*
11. any*
12. of *

Write each word you circled. Spell the word correctly.

1. _____ 2. _____

3. _____ 4. _____

Write an Explanation Think of all the care a pet needs. On a separate sheet of paper, write what you would do to take care of a pet. Use Spelling Words from the list.

Name _____

Means the Same

Word Bank

| hat | ship | bag | plate | wash | start |

In each ball, write a word from the box that means the same or almost the same as the word in the ball.

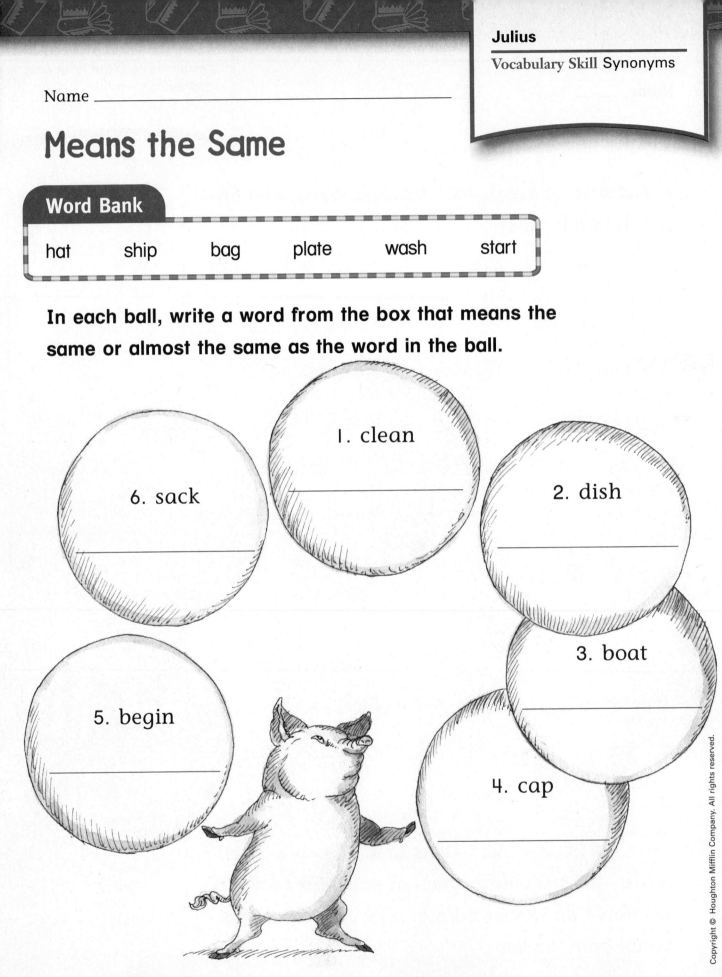

6. sack _____

1. clean _____

2. dish _____

3. boat _____

5. begin _____

4. cap _____

Copyright © Houghton Mifflin Company. All rights reserved.

Who or What?

► A sentence is a group of words that tells what someone or something did or does.

► The naming part of a sentence tells whom or what the sentence is about.

Word Bank

| milk | floor | mop | fox | cup |

**Look at the picture. Then read each sentence.
Write the naming part to complete the sentence.**

1. A _____ fell off the table.

2. The _____ spilled out.

3. The _____ has to clean up the mess.

4. A _____ will soak up the milk.

5. Then the _____ will be clean again.

Copyright © Houghton Mifflin Company. All rights reserved.

Name _____

Animal Manners

Word Bank

| fly | fox | bear | bees | kangaroo |

**Write the naming word from the box that rhymes
with the word in dark print in
the sentences below.**

1. These _____ say **please**
   when they ask for something.

2. A _____ asks what a
   guest would like to **do**.

3. The _____ says **good-bye**
   before hanging up the phone.

4. A _____ likes to **share**
   toys.

5. That _____ picks
   up his **socks**.

Copyright © Houghton Mifflin Company. All rights reserved.

Name _____

You're Last

Rewrite each of the sentences. Name yourself last.

1. I and Casey went swimming.

   _____

2. I and my friend are going to the movies.

   _____

3. I and my mother ate lunch at school.

   _____

Draw a picture of you and your friend doing something.

Write a sentence to go with your picture.

Name _____

Getting Ready to Respond

Use the chart to help you write a response journal entry about the story *Julius*.

What is the date?

_____

What is the title of the story?

_____

Who is the main character?

_____

What do you like best about the story?

_____

_____

Would you tell a friend to read the story?

_____

What example from the story explains why you like it?

_____

_____

Copyright © Houghton Mifflin Company. All rights reserved.

Name _____

Date It!

Rewrite the journal entry on the lines below. Write the circled words correctly.

(3 March 2001)

I read the story (Lost in the park.) The main

character in this story was Connor. My favorite part

was when he found his mother. I like it because (connor)

was brave. Even though he was scared, he didn't cry. I

am going to tell a friend to read this story because it

is a very good story.

_____

_____

_____

_____

_____

Copyright © Houghton Mifflin Company. All rights reserved.

Name _____

Long Vowel Game

**Read the sentences. Draw a circle around each word
that has a long vowel sound and that ends with silent *e*.**

1. We would like to play a game with you.

2. You count to five while we look for a place to hide.

3. When you count, you need to face the gate.

4. We can play until it is time to go inside.

**Now write each word you circled under the word that
has the same vowel sound and that ends with silent *e*.**

late	nine

Copyright © Houghton Mifflin Company. All rights reserved.

Chicken Riddle

Use words from the box to finish the sentences.

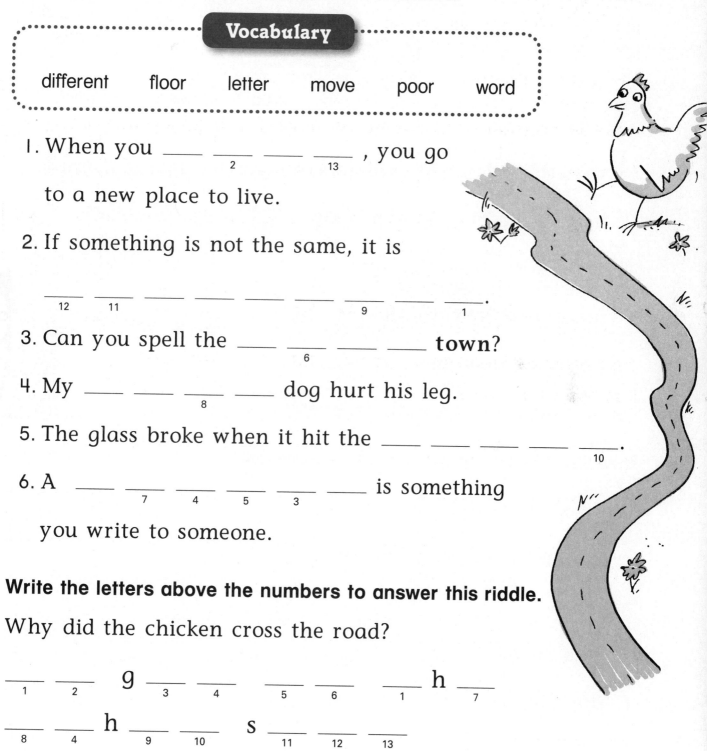

> ### Vocabulary
>
> different   floor   letter   move   poor   word

1. When you ___ ___ ___ ___ , you go

   2   13

   to a new place to live.

2. If something is not the same, it is

   ___ ___   ___ ___ .

   12   11   9   1

3. Can you spell the ___ ___ ___ ___ **town**?

   6

4. My ___ ___ ___ ___ dog hurt his leg.

   8

5. The glass broke when it hit the ___ ___ ___ ___ .

   10

6. A ___ ___ ___ ___ ___ is something

   7   4   5   3

   you write to someone.

Write the letters above the numbers to answer this riddle.

Why did the chicken cross the road?

___ ___ g ___ ___   ___ ___   ___ h ___

1   2   3   4   5   6   1   7

___ ___ h ___ ___   s ___ ___ ___

8   4   9   10   11 12 13

Copyright © Houghton Mifflin Company. All rights reserved.

Name _____

Picture the Vocabulary

Write each word from the box next to its correct definition.

> **Vocabulary**
>
> commotion   released   delivered   tired   feathers   wearing

1. something handed over to someone _____

2. having clothing on the body _____

3. light, soft parts of a bird _____

4. having set something free _____

5. noisy excitement _____

6. having little strength or energy _____

Now use the picture to finish these sentences.

7. As soon as the _____ was

   released, the **commotion** began. First,

   _____

   and then, _____

   and finally, _____

   _____

Copyright © Houghton Mifflin Company. All rights reserved.

Name _____

Prediction Chart

As you read the story, complete the chart.

What happens in the story?

_____

_____

_____

_____

What would happen if . . . ? _____

_____

Tell what happens. _____

_____

What would happen if . . . ? _____

_____

Tell what happens. _____

_____

Copyright © Houghton Mifflin Company. All rights reserved.

Theme 1: **Silly Stories**   45

Name _____

Story Time

Use the phrases in the box to complete the sentences.

> grabbed her feet   Mrs. Brown's house   in the barn out back
>
> crashed through the floor   to be good   go to the hospital

Saturday: Mrs. Brown rode away on her bicycle. As she went down the road, a dog _____. Mrs. Brown got hurt. She had to _____.

Monday: Mrs. Brown sent a letter. She told the animals _____. But the cow, pigs, ducks, and yak did not listen. They moved into _____.

Tuesday: When Mrs. Brown came home, she went to bed. She did not know that the cow, pigs, ducks, and yak were in her bed. Suddenly, the bed _____. They all went to the hospital. Soon it was time to go home. Now they all live together _____.

Copyright © Houghton Mifflin Company. All rights reserved.

Name _____

Predicting Outcomes

Read the story and then complete the chart on the next page.

Pets in a Classroom

Mr. Clark's class was excited today. The children had brought their pets to school. There were three little dogs, one puppy, two cats, two kittens, one parrot, two goldfish, one lizard, one snake, two hamsters, one turtle, one rabbit, and even one chicken. The animals sat quietly while Mr. Clark talked about each of them.

At lunchtime the children left the animals in the classroom. As soon as the door was closed, the animals got into trouble. The dogs chased the cats. The hamsters and turtle ate the children's work. The puppy tried to catch the parrot, and the kittens tried to catch the fish. The rabbit knocked over some paint, and it spilled onto the lizard. The snake crawled into Mr. Clark's desk, and the chicken laid an egg on top of it!

When the class got back from lunch, the children saw the mess. But Mr. Clark did not notice.

Copyright © Houghton Mifflin Company. All rights reserved.

Theme 1: **Silly Stories**   47

Name _____

Predicting Outcomes continued

After you read the story, complete the chart below.

What happens in the story?

1. _____

2. _____

3. _____

4. _____

What would happen if . . . ? _____

_____

Tell what happens. _____

_____

What would happen if . . . ? _____

_____

Tell what happens. _____

_____

Copyright © Houghton Mifflin Company. All rights reserved.

Name _____

Vowel Sound Bubbles

Read each word aloud. Listen for the vowel sound.

Color bubbles that have words with a short *o* sound yellow.

Color bubbles that have words with a short *u* sound blue.

Color bubbles that have words with a short *e* sound green.

went

dusting

frog

ducks

tested

drops

just

ten

hospital

butter

Copyright © Houghton Mifflin Company. All rights reserved.

Name _____

Sorting Spelling Words

Ten Spelling Words have a long vowel sound and end with silent *e*. The words **give** and **have** do not follow this rule. The letters follow the pattern, but the words do not have long vowel sounds.

Write each word in the box under the word with the same vowel sound.

Spelling Words

1. bite
2. late
3. size
4. made
5. side
6. ate
7. fine
8. same
9. hide
10. line
11. give*
12. have*

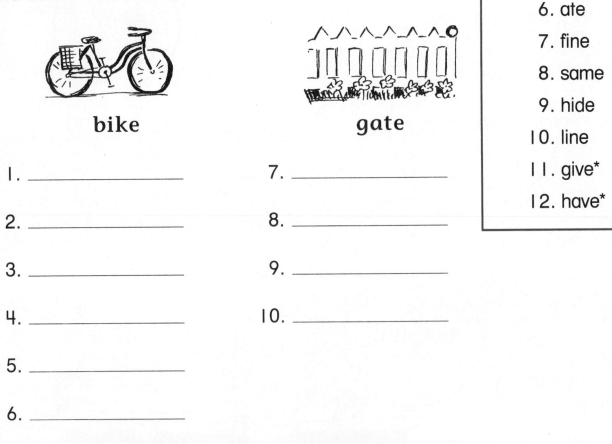

bike

1. _____

2. _____

3. _____

4. _____

5. _____

6. _____

gate

7. _____

8. _____

9. _____

10. _____

Write the Spelling Word that answers each question.

11. Which word rhymes with **live**? _____

12. Which word starts with a vowel? _____

Copyright © Houghton Mifflin Company. All rights reserved.

Name _____

Spelling Spree

Unscramble the letters in each Spelling Word. Write the word on the line.

1. elin _____

2. ahve _____

3. ltae _____

4. eta _____

5. sdei _____

6. maes _____

7. dame _____

8. idhe _____

9. vige _____

10. zies _____

11. nfie _____

12. iteb _____

Spelling Words

1. bite
2. late
3. size
4. made
5. side
6. ate
7. fine
8. same
9. hide
10. line
11. give*
12. have*

Copyright © Houghton Mifflin Company. All rights reserved.

Name _____

Proofreading and Writing

Proofreading Find and circle four Spelling Words that are spelled wrong in this puppet show. Write each word correctly.

Spelling Words

Mouse: I made a cake for Beth.

Duck: Great! We can givve it to her when she gets home.

Mouse: Look at the cake! Someone took a bitt out of this side.

Duck: It looks fien to me.

Mouse: Maybe I should cut that piece off and make the cake a smaller siz.

Duck: I have a better idea. Let's eat this cake and make a new one for Beth.

1. bite
2. late
3. size
4. made
5. side
6. ate
7. fine
8. same
9. hide
10. line
11. give*
12. have*

_____   _____

_____   _____

Write an Opinion Write a few sentences telling what you think happened to the cake. Use another sheet of paper. Use Spelling Words from your list.

Copyright © Houghton Mifflin Company. All rights reserved.

Name _____

Word Meanings

Read the two meanings for each word. Then write a sentence for each meaning. The first one has been done for you.

Example: land

    The **land** is the ground.

    To **land** is to come down.

The farmer's land is flat.

We watch the plane land.

back

    The **back** is the rear part of the body.

    To come **back** is to return.

1. _____

2. _____

tire

    A **tire** is a circle of rubber.

    To **tire** is to get sleepy.

3. _____

4. _____

Copyright © Houghton Mifflin Company. All rights reserved.

Name _____

Action Parts Puzzle

Color red the puzzle pieces with action parts.

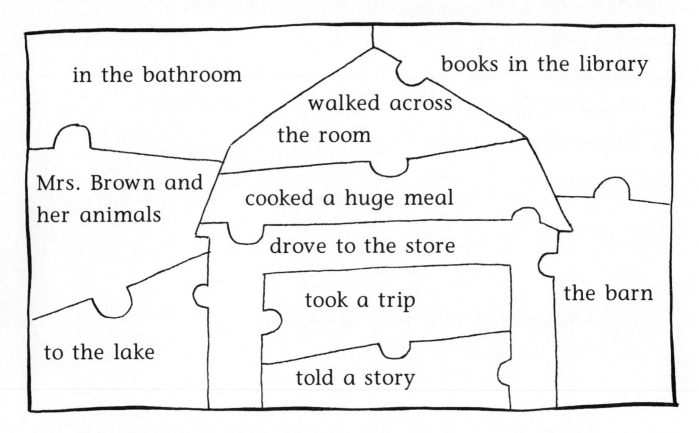

in the bathroom

books in the library

walked across the room

Mrs. Brown and her animals

cooked a huge meal

drove to the store

took a trip

the barn

to the lake

told a story

Now write complete sentences for the puzzle parts that you colored red.

1. _____

2. _____

3. _____

4. _____

5. _____

Copyright © Houghton Mifflin Company. All rights reserved.

Animal Actions

Complete each sentence to tell what the animals are doing.
Be sure to put a period at the end of each sentence.

> purrs as it naps under a tree   barks at the ducks
> trot across the field to the barn   quack loudly
> hops on the lily pads in the pond

1. Some horses _____

_____

2. The ducks in the pond _____

_____

3. The frog _____

_____

4. A big brown dog _____

_____

5. The cat _____

_____

Copyright © Houghton Mifflin Company. All rights reserved.

Name _____

Listing Actions

Here is a list of things the animals did while Mrs. Brown was gone.
Circle *Yes* or *No* to tell whether each item has an action part.

What the Animals Did

1. One of her gowns.   Yes   No

2. The yak and cow.   Yes   No

3. The ducks rang the doorbell   Yes   No
   many times.

4. The pigs painted the house.   Yes   No

5. A snack from food in the pantry.   Yes   No

Add words to the items that did not have action parts. Write
the complete sentences on the lines below.

_____

_____

_____

_____

_____

Copyright © Houghton Mifflin Company. All rights reserved.

Name _____

Organizing a Journal Entry

What is the date of the journal entry?

What happened to me that I want to write about?

Who was there? What did they say?

Who	⟶	What They Said

What happened?   What describing words tell about the events?

Events	→	Describing Words

Copyright © Houghton Mifflin Company. All rights reserved.

Name _____

Goldilocks's Journal

After Goldilocks visited the three bears, she wrote this plan for a journal entry. On a separate sheet of paper, write your own journal entry. Use this plan to help you.

Date

What do I want to write about?

Who was there?   What did they say?

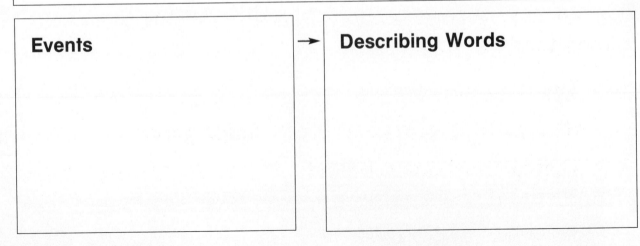

Who ⟶ **What They Said**

Events ⟶ **Describing Words**

Copyright © Houghton Mifflin Company. All rights reserved.

Name _____

Choosing the Best Answer

Use what you have learned about taking tests to help you answer these questions. You may go back to **Dragon Gets By** if you need to. This practice will help you when you take this kind of test.

Read each question. Choose the best answer. Fill in the circle beside your answer.

1 Where is Dragon at the beginning of the story?

  ○ at the store

  ○ at home

  ○ in his car

2 Why does Dragon go to the store?

  ○ He loves to shop for different kinds of food.

  ○ He is a wise shopper.

  ○ He doesn't have any food in his cupboard.

3 What happens when Dragon tries to put the food that he bought in his car?

  ○ The food does not fit.

  ○ He sees that he forgot to buy fudge pops.

  ○ The car rolls down the hill.

Copyright © Houghton Mifflin Company. All rights reserved.

Name _____

Choosing the Best Answer

continued

4 Where is Dragon when he eats all the food he bought?

- ○ at home
- ○ in the parking lot
- ○ in the store

5 Why can't Dragon fit in his car?

- ○ He ate too much food.
- ○ He had too many bags of food.
- ○ He grew too tall.

6 At the end of the story, what does Dragon find when he opens his cupboard?

- ○ The cupboard is full of food.
- ○ His car is in the cupboard.
- ○ The cupboard is still empty.

Copyright © Houghton Mifflin Company. All rights reserved.

Name _____

Spelling Review

Write Spelling Words from the list to answer the questions.

1–14. Which words have the short **a**, **e**, **i**, **o**, or **u** sound?

1. _____   8. _____

2. _____   9. _____

3. _____   10. _____

4. _____   11. _____

5. _____   12. _____

6. _____   13. _____

7. _____   14. _____

15–20. Which words have the long **a** or long **i** sound?

15. _____   18. _____

16. _____   19. _____

17. _____   20. _____

Spelling Words

1. am
2. hide
3. made
4. his
5. nut
6. dig
7. job
8. size
9. fox
10. sat
10. fun
12. late
13. hug
14. wet
14. mop
16. went
17. leg
18. bite
19. ran
20. ate

Copyright © Houghton Mifflin Company. All rights reserved.

Theme 1: **Silly Stories**   61

Name _____

Spelling Spree

Silly Scramble Change the order of letters in the words below to make Spelling Words.

1. tale _____

2. eat _____

3. gel _____

4. dame _____

Spelling Words

1. went
2. bite
3. ran
4. fox
5. made
6. ate
7. nut
8. late
9. leg
10. fun

Rhyme Time Finish the sentences. Write a Spelling Word that rhymes with the word in dark print.

5. Mom and I _____ to buy a new **tent**.

6. I saw a _____ peek out of the **box**.

7. A hungry bird took a _____ from my **kite**.

8. Jason _____ to get a **pan**.

9. Just for _____, let's draw a red **sun**!

10. I found a _____ inside of a **hut**.

Copyright © Houghton Mifflin Company. All rights reserved.

Name _____

Proofreading and Writing

Proofreading **Circle four Spelling Words below that are wrong. Then write them correctly.**

Copyright © Houghton Mifflin Company. All rights reserved.

I yam a squirrel named Sam. I like to play with my friend Tree. I give her a big hugg each day. We have lots of fun. I hied in her branches. She always finds me! When it is wett, she keeps me dry.

<table>
<tr><td>Spelling Words</td></tr>
<tr><td>1. dig</td></tr>
<tr><td>2. wet</td></tr>
<tr><td>3. sat</td></tr>
<tr><td>4. his</td></tr>
<tr><td>5. mop</td></tr>
<tr><td>6. job</td></tr>
<tr><td>7. hide</td></tr>
<tr><td>8. size</td></tr>
<tr><td>9. am</td></tr>
<tr><td>10. hug</td></tr>
</table>

1. _____   3. _____

2. _____   4. _____

Finish the Story **Write Spelling Words to complete the sentences in this story.**

Sam the squirrel 5. _____ in Tree. He ate 6. _____ last nut. He would have to 7. _____ up more later. Today's 8. _____ was to clean up under Tree. "Tree," Sam asked, "where is the 9. _____ ?"

"You can't use that!" Tree said. "You're too small in 10. _____ ."

Finish the Story **On another sheet of paper, write a letter from Tree. Use the Spelling Review words.**

Name _____

Nature Walk

**What about nature and the outdoors do you enjoy most?
Describe an event or activity that you have seen or enjoyed
doing outdoors.**

_____

_____

_____

_____

_____

_____

_____

**Complete the word web with words and phrases that describe a
nature walk you have taken.**

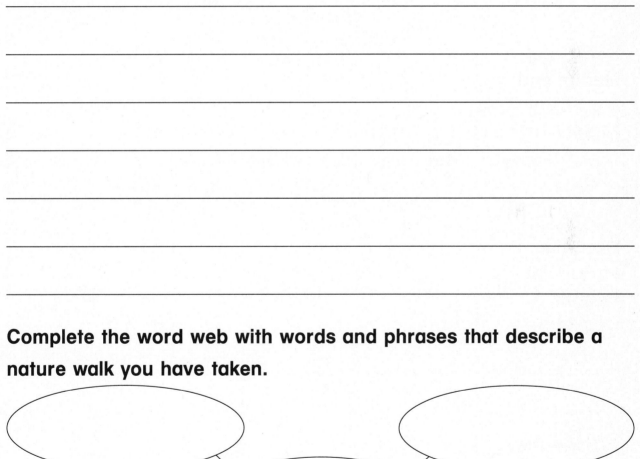

A Nature Walk

Copyright © Houghton Mifflin Company. All rights reserved.

Name _____

Nature Walk

Fill in the chart as you read the stories.

	Where does the nature walk in the story take place?	What do some of the characters see and learn about on their nature walk?
Henry and Mudge and the Starry Night		
Exploring Parks with Ranger Dockett		
Around the Pond: Who's Been Here?		

Copyright © Houghton Mifflin Company. All rights reserved.

Name _____

Go Long

Say the name of each picture. Circle the picture of the
word that has the long vowel sound and a silent *e* at the end.

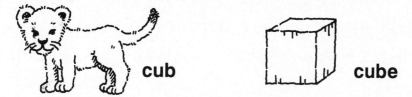

cub   cube

**Complete each pair of sentences using the words
in the boxes.**

1. My _____ is part of my face.

   My teacher wrote me a _____.

nose   note

2. It is not polite to be _____ to
   other people.
   Follow every school _____.

rule   rude

3. My brother's name is _____.

   _____ are my socks.

These   Pete

4. The flag is on the _____.

   Byron told a funny _____.

pole   joke

5. The store is _____.

   Are you _____ today?

closing voting

Copyright © Houghton Mifflin Company. All rights reserved.

Name _____

Tiger and Giraffe Sounds

There are two sounds for the letter **g**. It can sound like the **g** in the middle of  , or it can sound like the **g** at the beginning of ![giraffe] .

Copyright © Houghton Mifflin Company. All rights reserved.

Word Bank

gift	gym	huge	page	village
pig	flag	gave	giant	wagon

Write each word from the box under the word that has the matching *g* sound.

Tiger

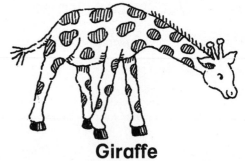

Giraffe

1. _____

2. _____

3. _____

4. _____

5. _____

6. _____

7. _____

8. _____

9. _____

10. _____

68 Theme 2: **Nature Walk**

Name _____

Puzzle Play

Fill in the puzzle with words from the box that fit the clues.

Word Bank

| quiet | even | straight | beautiful | year |

Across

1. Last _____ we went camping at Star Lake.
2. It is so _____ there.
3. At night it is very _____.

Down

4. You cannot _____ hear a bird chirping.
5. As soon as it gets dark I go _____ to sleep!

Think of a quiet and beautiful place. Write a sentence about it.

6. _____

_____

_____

Copyright © Houghton Mifflin Company. All rights reserved.

Name _____

Camping Words

Use words from the box to label the pictures.

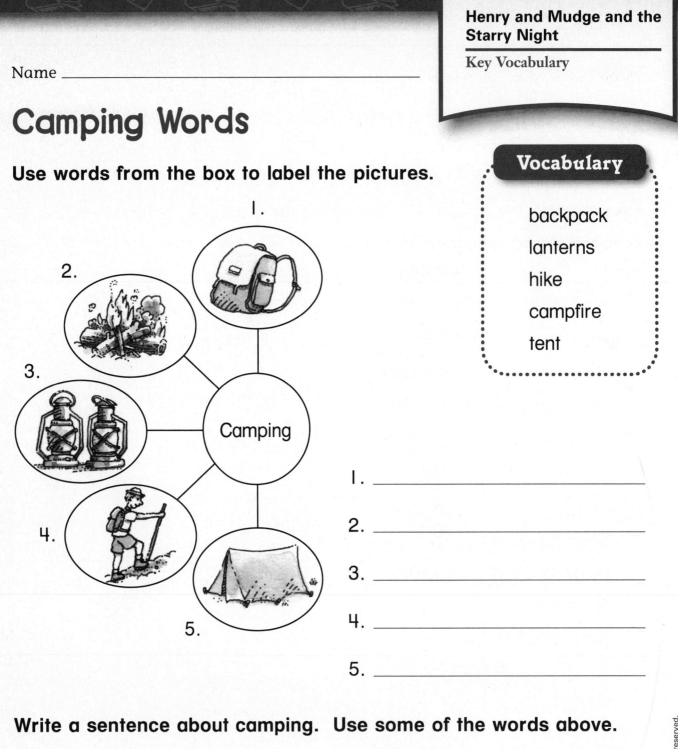

Vocabulary

backpack

lanterns

hike

campfire

tent

1. _____

2. _____

3. _____

4. _____

5. _____

Write a sentence about camping. Use some of the words above.

6. _____

_____

_____

Copyright © Houghton Mifflin Company. All rights reserved.

Name _____

Graphic Organizer

Venn Diagram As you read the story, write what Henry's mother is like, what Henry's father is like, and how both are the same.

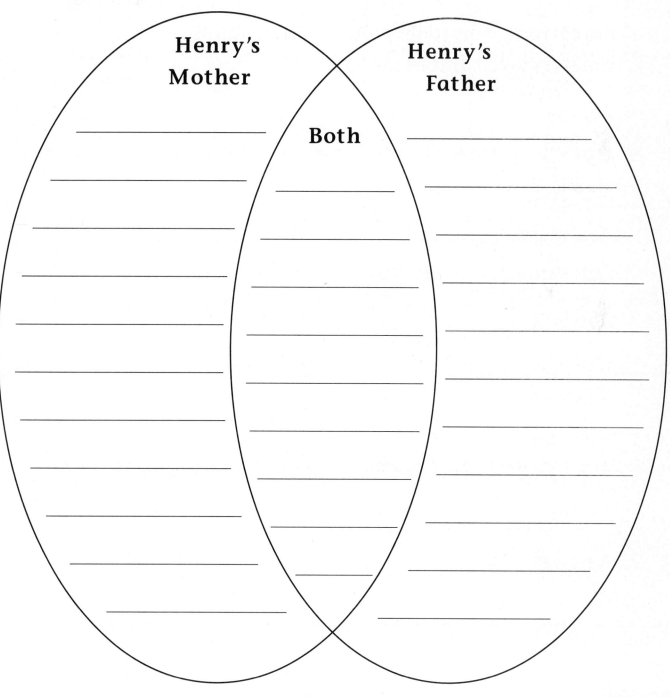

Copyright © Houghton Mifflin Company. All rights reserved.

Name _____

Interviewing Henry

**Write the answers Henry might
give to these questions.**

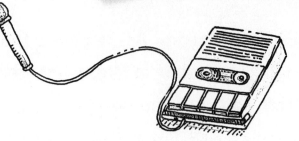

1. **Question:** Why does your mother know so
much about camping?

Answer: _____

2. **Question:** How did Mudge know you had a
cookie in your back pocket?

Answer: _____

3. **Question:** How did you cook your food?

Answer: _____

4. **Question:** What did your mother see in the
night sky?

Answer: _____

5. **Question:** Why did you and your family have
"green" dreams while camping?

Answer: _____

_____

Copyright © Houghton Mifflin Company. All rights reserved.

Name _____

Compare and Contrast

Read the story. Complete the diagram on page 74.

Alike and Different

Lori and her parents like the outdoors. One sunny Saturday, the family decided to go hiking at a nearby park. They dressed in their hiking clothes and got their backpacks. Mom put food in her backpack. She told Lori that they would have a picnic lunch. Dad packed a picnic blanket, the first-aid kit, and the park map in his backpack. Lori put only one thing in her backpack. It was her cat, Sprinkles!

The family walked to the park with Sprinkles peeking out from Lori's backpack. In the park, Mom and Dad waved to other hikers they passed. Dad talked about the plants they saw. He knew a lot about plants. Mom looked over her shoulder to check on Lori and Sprinkles.

After a while, the family stopped to rest. Sprinkles took a nap. Mom pointed to some wild animals she saw. Suddenly, Dad decided to be silly. He pretended to be the animals. He scampered like a squirrel, hopped like a rabbit, and flapped his arms like a bird. Lori and her mom laughed.

Copyright © Houghton Mifflin Company. All rights reserved.

Name _____

Compare and Contrast
(continued)

Think about the story you read. Then fill in the chart to tell how Lori's mother and father are alike and different.

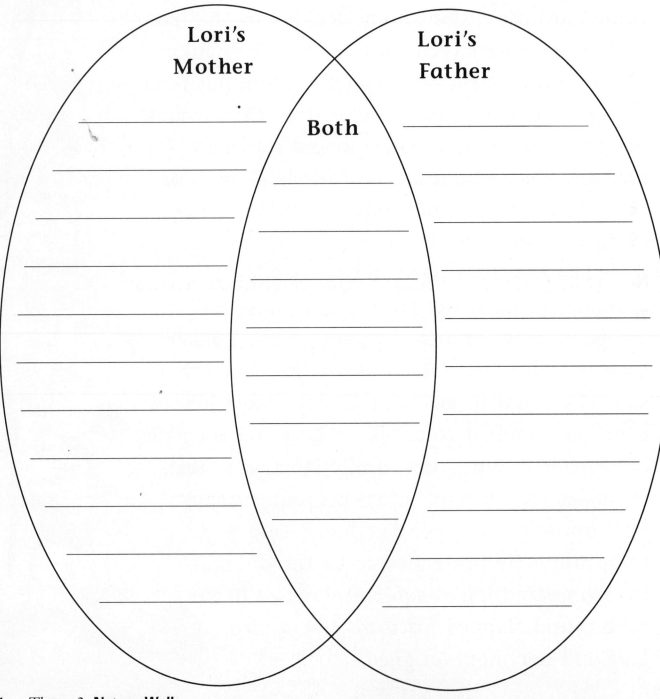

Copyright © Houghton Mifflin Company. All rights reserved.

Name _____

Fishing for Vowels

**Read the sentences. Draw a circle around each word
that has a long vowel sound and that ends with silent *e*.**

1. My friend and I live by the lake.
2. We are both nine years old.
3. We are about the same size.
4. I usually sleep late.
5. He comes to wake me up.
6. Then we go fishing and play hide and seek.
7. Sometimes we race our toy cars.
8. My friend is nice.
9. I like him very much.

**Now write each word you circled in the fish that has the
same vowel sound and a silent *e* at the end.**

safe

hide

Copyright © Houghton Mifflin Company. All rights reserved.

Name _____

Match the Sound

Most of the Spelling Words have the long vowel sound and end with silent *e*.

► The words **one** and **goes** do not follow this rule.

Write each Spelling Word under the word with the same vowel sound and a silent *e* at the end.

Spelling Words

1. bone
2. robe
3. use
4. these
5. rope
6. note
7. cute
8. close
9. hope
10. those
11. one*
12. goes*

Home

_____

_____

_____

_____

_____

_____

Cube

_____

_____

Pete

_____

Write one word that does not have the long vowel sound. Write one word with a long vowel sound that does not end with silent *e*.

_____   _____

Copyright © Houghton Mifflin Company. All rights reserved.

Name _____

Spelling Spree

Write a Spelling Word for each clue.

1. It rhymes with **flute**.
   It begins like **cup**. _____

2. It rhymes with **nose**.
   It begins like **get**. _____

3. It rhymes with **hose**.
   It begins like **clock**. _____

4. It rhymes with **cone**.
   It begins like **bat**. _____

5. It rhymes with **keys**.
   It begins like **them**. _____

6. It rhymes with **soap**.
   It begins like **home**. _____

7. It rhymes with **boat**.
   It begins like **name**. _____

8. It rhymes with **rose**.
   It begins like **that**. _____

Copyright © Houghton Mifflin Company. All rights reserved.

Spelling Words

1. bone
2. robe
3. use
4. these
5. rope
6. note
7. cute
8. close
9. hope
10. those
11. one*
12. goes*

Name _____

Proofreading and Writing

Here is a letter Henry might have written. Circle four Spelling Words that are not spelled correctly. Write them correctly on the lines.

Spelling Words

1. bone
2. robe
3. use
4. these
5. rope
6. note
7. cute
8. close
9. hope
10. those
11. one*
12. goes*

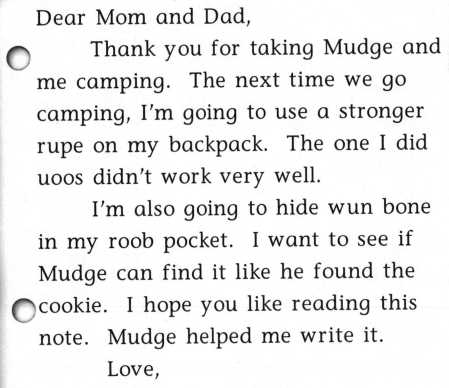

Dear Mom and Dad,

Thank you for taking Mudge and me camping. The next time we go camping, I'm going to use a stronger rupe on my backpack. The one I did uoos didn't work very well.

I'm also going to hide wun bone in my roob pocket. I want to see if Mudge can find it like he found the cookie. I hope you like reading this note. Mudge helped me write it.

Love,

Henry and Mudge

Henry

_____   _____

_____   _____

Write a Note On another sheet of paper, write a note to someone. Use Spelling Words from the list.

Copyright © Houghton Mifflin Company. All rights reserved.

Name _____

One + One = One

A **compound word** is made up of two shorter
words. The word **campfire** is a compound word.

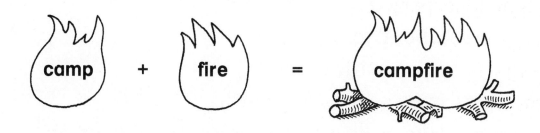

camp + fire = campfire

**Draw a line from the word on the left to the word on the
right to make a compound word.**

1. sun	storm
2. thunder	rise
3. water	bow
4. rain	fall

Now use each compound word in a sentence.

5. _____

6. _____

7. _____

8. _____

Copyright © Houghton Mifflin Company. All rights reserved.

Name _____

Sentence or Question?

▶ A telling sentence tells about someone or something. It begins with a capital letter and ends with a period.

▶ A question asks about someone or something. It begins with a capital letter and ends with a question mark.

Unscramble the words to make a telling sentence or a question.
Remember to use capital letters and the correct end marks.

1. fun is camping _____

    _____

2. sleep a we in tent _____

    _____

3. like you go camping to do _____

    _____

Write a telling sentence about the picture.

4. _____

    _____

Write a question about the picture.

5. _____

    _____

Copyright © Houghton Mifflin Company. All rights reserved.

Name _____

Sentence to Question

Read each telling sentence. Turn it into a question.
Use words from the box. The first one has been
done for you.

Word Bank

Where

Who

When

What

1. Some people love to go camping.

   What do some people love to do?
   _____

2. It is fun to go camping in the summer.

   _____

3. My dad likes to sleep in a tent.

   _____

4. I like to go camping at Star Lake.

   _____

What can you do on a camping trip? Write two telling sentences.

5. _____

   _____

   _____

Copyright © Houghton Mifflin Company. All rights reserved.

Name _____

Change It!

**Change these telling sentences to questions.
Remember to begin with a capital letter
and include the correct end mark.**

1. Henry and Mudge went camping in August.

_____

2. Mudge is Henry's big dog.

_____

3. Henry's parents took Henry and Mudge camping.

_____

_____

**Change these questions into telling sentences. Remember to
begin with a capital letter and include the correct end mark.**

4. Did Mudge have a backpack?

_____

5. Did Henry want to see a bear?

_____

_____

6. Did Henry and his family go hiking?

_____

Copyright © Houghton Mifflin Company. All rights reserved.

Name _____

Questions and Answers

Write an answer to each question. Remember to write complete sentences.

1. **Question:** Where did Henry and his family go camping?

   Answer: _____

   _____

2. **Question:** What did Mudge carry in his backpack?

   Answer: _____

   _____

3. **Question:** What did Henry's father bring with him?

   Answer: _____

   _____

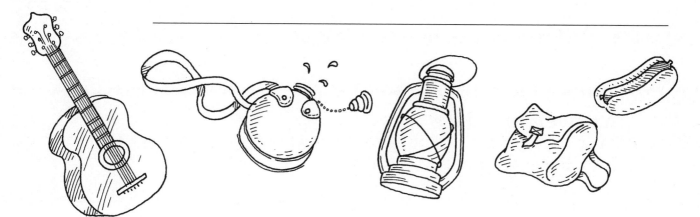

Copyright © Houghton Mifflin Company. All rights reserved.

Name _____

What Do You See?

**Look at the picture. Read the questions and answers.
Rewrite the answers to make them complete sentences.**

1. **Question:** Which animals are sleeping in the cave?
   Answer: the bears

   _____

   _____

2. **Question:** What are the raccoons doing?
   Answer: catching fish

   _____

   _____

3. **Question:** What is the bird doing?
   Answer: sitting in a tree

   _____

   _____

4. **Question:** Which animal is standing under a tree?
   Answer: the deer

   _____

   _____

Copyright © Houghton Mifflin Company. All rights reserved.

Name _____

Revising Your Description

Put a check next to the sentences that tell about your writing.

Superstar

☐ I told the reader what I am describing.

☐ My description tells how something looks, feels, sounds, tastes, and smells.

☐ My description uses details to make a clear picture for the reader.

☐ I wrote in complete sentences.

Rising Star

☐ I need to tell what I am describing.

☐ I need to add words that tell how something looks, feels, sounds, tastes, and smells.

☐ I could add some details to make a clearer picture for the reader.

☐ Some of my sentences are not complete.

Copyright © Houghton Mifflin Company. All rights reserved.

Name _____

Writing Sentences

Read each group of words. Write the group of words that is a sentence.

1. All kinds of people come to the river.
   All kinds of people.

   _____

2. In the river.
   My dad likes to catch fish in the river.

   _____

3. Different birds and bugs.
   I see different birds and bugs here.

   _____

4. Life on the river changes from season to season.
   From season to season.

   _____

Think of an outdoor spot you enjoy. Write two sentences about it. Make sure your sentence tells what someone or something is doing.

5. _____

6. _____

Copyright © Houghton Mifflin Company. All rights reserved.

Spelling Words

These Spelling Words are words that you use in your writing. Look carefully at how they are spelled. Write the missing letters in the Spelling Words below. Use the words in the box.

1. o____

2. w_____t

3. a____

4. h_____

5. c_____e

6. ____f

7. fr____m

8. d_____s

9. h_____

10. th____r____

11. g_____s

12. the_____

Spelling Words

1. on
2. am
3. come
4. if
5. does
6. goes
7. from
8. his
9. want
10. her
11. their
12. there

Write the Spelling Words below.

_____   _____

_____   _____

_____   _____

_____   _____

_____   _____

Copyright © Houghton Mifflin Company. All rights reserved.

Name _____

Spelling Spree

Write a Spelling Word to finish each riddle.

Spelling Words

1. on
2. am
3. come
4. if
5. does
6. goes
7. from
8. his
9. want
10. her
11. their
12. there

1. I'm made _____ wood.
   You can write with me.

2. I swim _____ in the lake.
   I have scales and fins.

3. I _____ out at night.
   I rhyme with soon.

4. I _____ on a wall.
   You can see yourself in me.

5. I am _____ best friend.
   She likes me.
   I bark and run.

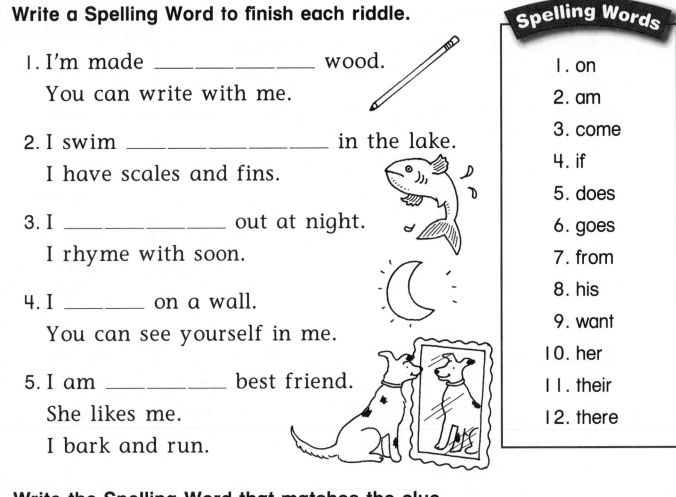

Write the Spelling Word that matches the clue.

6. the opposite of **off**   _____

7. to do something   _____

8. to go somewhere   _____

9. to wish for something   _____

10. shows something belongs
    to some people   _____

Copyright © Houghton Mifflin Company. All rights reserved.

Name _____

Proofreading and Writing

Proofreading Find and circle misspelled Spelling
Words below. Then write each word correctly.

The little bird landed on the fence
post. He had cume from the woods. His
feathers were brown with speckles of black.
"Ef he is hungry, he will wunt the seeds," I
thought.

Suddenly he swooped down onto the
deck. He pecked the tiny, hard seeds I had
thrown thair. Suddenly, he lifted hiz head
as if he heard a sound. He flapped his
wings and flew off into the woods.

Spelling Words

1. on
2. am
3. come
4. if
5. does
6. goes
7. from
8. his
9. want
10. her
11. their
12. there

_____ _____

_____ _____

_____

✏️ **Write and Draw an Animal** On another
sheet of paper, draw pictures of some animals
you might see in your backyard. Write a
sentence below each picture that tells about the
animal. Use as many Spelling Words as you can.

Copyright © Houghton Mifflin Company. All rights reserved.

Name That!

**Write the name of each picture. Then circle the
consonant cluster.**

Example:

(present)

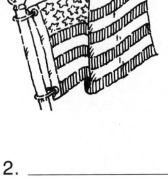

1. _____

2. _____

3. _____

4. _____

5. _____

6. _____

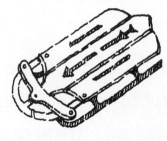

7. _____

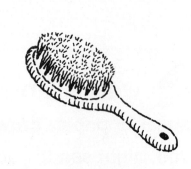

8. _____

90   Theme 2: **Nature Walk**

Copyright © Houghton Mifflin Company. All rights reserved.

Name _____

Camping Trip

Read the story. Circle the words in which the letter *c* makes the same sound you hear at the beginning of the word *sand*.

Juan and Hal went to the park to camp. They were far from the city. They carried their equipment to the pond and set up their tent near a fence. It was a cold night, so they collected wood and made a big fire. Their faces glowed in the firelight. They cooked hot dogs. Then they ate cookies and went to sleep. In the morning there was a thin layer of ice on the pond. But Juan and Hal were warm in their tent!

Now read the story again. Draw a line under the words in which *c* makes the same sound you hear at the beginning of *cup*.

Copyright © Houghton Mifflin Company. All rights reserved.

Name _____

A Ranger's Day

Read what one park ranger did at work today.

Then answer the questions.

10:00 Collect seeds to plant later this week.

12:30 Eat lunch with the other rangers.

2:00 Check on the baby deer at the
petting zoo.

3:00 *Important: Take class to plant trees.

5:00 Go home after this busy day!

1. How did the park ranger stay in touch with the
other rangers?

_____

_____

2. What young animals did he check on?

_____

_____

3. When will the seeds be planted?

_____

_____

4. What kind of day did the park ranger have?

_____

Copyright © Houghton Mifflin Company. All rights reserved.

Name _____

A Special Job

Use words from the box to finish the sentences. They will tell about a very special job.

Vocabulary

exploring   habitat   protect   ranger   tours   urban

1. A park _____ has many jobs.

2. Some rangers work in _____ parks.

3. They lead people on _____ to see plants and animals.

4. Rangers must know many things about the _____ around them.

5. They must enjoy _____ the natural world.

6. It is their job to _____ the plants and animals.

Copyright © Houghton Mifflin Company. All rights reserved.

Name _____

K-W-L Chart

Complete this chart.

What I Know

Rangers take care of parks.

_____

_____

_____

_____

What I Learned

_____

_____

_____

_____

What I Want to Know

_____

_____

_____

_____

Copyright © Houghton Mifflin Company. All rights reserved.

Describe the Job

Read the want ad. Write a word to complete each sentence.

Park Ranger Needed!

Central Park needs a new ranger. To do this job well, you must be able to lead people on

_____ of the park. You must keep

in _____ with other rangers. You

must _____ trees, help people follow

the park _____, and teach classes

about the plants and _____ found in the park.

What kind of person would make a good park ranger? Finish this sentence.

A good park ranger is someone who

_____

_____

_____

_____

Copyright © Houghton Mifflin Company. All rights reserved.

Name _____

Fact and Opinion

Read the story. Answer the questions on page 97.

The Park in Winter

The park is a fun place to go in the winter. When the pond freezes, it is a good place to ice skate. There is a small building by the pond. Inside the building it is nice and warm. You can even buy delicious hot chocolate there.

When it snows, bring your sled. The hill is a good place for sledding. The snow on the hill is soft and deep. Be careful around the trees. You don't want to crash! Sometimes there are twenty children sledding on the hill. They wear hats, gloves, and boots to stay warm. Their sleds are red, green, blue, and yellow. There are so many colors! Sledding is fun for everyone.

Right after the snow falls, the park is very quiet. The snow helps to make it quiet. But if you listen, you might hear a woodpecker pecking an old tree. It is looking for bugs to eat. A busy woodpecker is noisy.

Copyright © Houghton Mifflin Company. All rights reserved.

Name _____

Fact and Opinion (continued)

Think about what you read. Then write facts or opinions from the story.

Write one fact about the building.

_____

Write an opinion about hot chocolate.

_____

Write one fact about the children sledding.

_____

Write an opinion about sledding.

_____

Write one fact about woodpeckers.

_____

Write one opinion about woodpeckers.

_____

What do you like about the park in winter?
Write one fact and one opinion.

Fact: _____

Opinion: _____

Copyright © Houghton Mifflin Company. All rights reserved.

Vowel Fun

**Draw a circle around each word that has a long vowel
sound and that ends with silent *e*.**

some   home

holes   poke   these

hear   huge   love

went   cute

Use the words you circled to finish these sentences.

1. The park is _____ to many
   animals.

2. Once I saw a _____ little frog.

3. Some birds live in _____ in
   the trees.

4. I passed a turtle that started to
   _____ its head out of its shell.

5. A horse was standing next to a
   _____ tree.

6. All _____ animals make the park
   a fun place.

Copyright © Houghton Mifflin Company. All rights reserved.

Name _____

Consonant Clusters

A **consonant cluster** is two consonant letters whose sounds are blended together. Some consonant clusters are **tr**, **sw**, **st**, **cl**, **xt**, **br**, and **gl**.

Spelling Words

1. trip
2. swim
3. step
4. nest
5. club
6. stone
7. next
8. brave
9. glad
10. lost

Write the Spelling Words that begin with a consonant cluster.

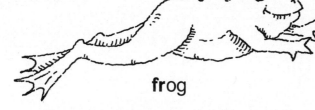

frog

_____ _____

_____ _____

_____

Write the Spelling Words that end with a consonant cluster.

bi**rd**

_____ _____

_____

Copyright © Houghton Mifflin Company. All rights reserved.

Name _____

Spelling Spree

Combine letters from the two frogs to make the Spelling Words that begin with two consonants.

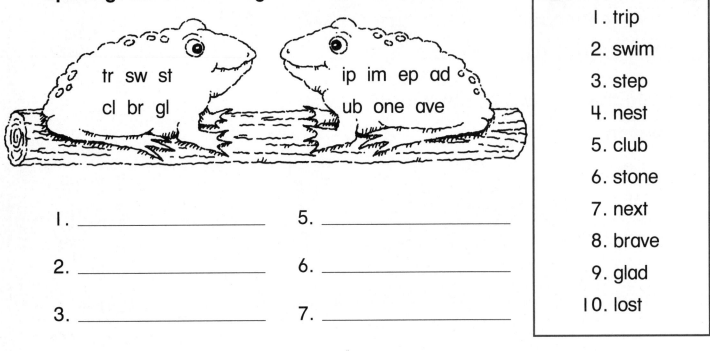

tr sw st
cl br gl

ip im ep ad
ub one ave

Spelling Words

1. trip
2. swim
3. step
4. nest
5. club
6. stone
7. next
8. brave
9. glad
10. lost

1. _____
2. _____
3. _____
4. _____

5. _____
6. _____
7. _____

Combine letters from the two birds to make Spelling Words that end with two consonants.

ne lo

st xt

8. _____
9. _____

10. _____

Copyright © Houghton Mifflin Company. All rights reserved.

Name _____

Proofreading and Writing

Proofreading Read the sentences below. Find three Spelling Words that are not spelled correctly. Draw a circle around the words. Then write each word correctly.

What to do on the class field trip:

1. Look for a nets.

2. Look under a ston for bugs.

3. Find the place where the fish smim.

Spelling Words

1. trip
2. swim
3. step
4. nest
5. club
6. stone
7. next
8. brave
9. glad
10. lost

1. _____

2. _____

3. _____

Writing What kinds of things does a bird do? Write two sentences about a bird. Use some of your Spelling Words in your sentences.

_____

_____

_____

Copyright © Houghton Mifflin Company. All rights reserved.

Name _____

Match the Opposites

Draw a line from each word on the left to a word on the right that has the opposite meaning.

1. sad   found

2. lost   finish

3. never   happy

4. thick   thin

5. below   always

6. start   above

Think of words that mean the opposite of each of the words below. Write those words on the lines.

7. front _____   9. dark _____

8. soft _____   10. asleep _____

Copyright © Houghton Mifflin Company. All rights reserved.

Name _____

Find the Commands

A command

► is a sentence that tells someone what to do

► has an understood subject **you**

► begins with a capital letter and ends with a period

**Read the sentences below. If a sentence is a
command, write C on the line next to it.**

_____ 1. Who likes to go to the park?

_____ 2. Dogs run in the park.

_____ 3. Keep your dog on a leash.

_____ 4. Don't throw balls near the pond.

_____ 5. The park is always open.

_____ 6. Don't pick the flowers.

_____ 7. Some people like to run in the park.

_____ 8. Keep your bike on the trail.

_____ 9. When can we meet the park ranger?

_____ 10. Use the trash cans.

Copyright © Houghton Mifflin Company. All rights reserved.

Name _____

Command Some Fun

Read each sentence about the park. Then change it into a command.

1. I want you to have fun in the park.

_____

2. You can meet the other park rangers at noon.

_____

3. I think you should listen to the birds.

_____

4. Everyone can take a picture of the deer.

_____

5. You should stay on the trail.

_____

Copyright © Houghton Mifflin Company. All rights reserved.

Name _____

Use Good Manners

Read this note that a park ranger wrote.
Look for places to make it more polite.

We are going on a field trip to the pond. Be ready for a big adventure. This trip will be fun. Wear rubber boots or old shoes. Your feet might get wet. Bring a sweater or jacket. The air is cool in the fall. Don't bring any more than you need. But bring a smile!

Write the note again. Add the word *please* in five places.
Use capital letters and end marks correctly.

_____

_____

_____

_____

_____

_____

_____

Copyright © Houghton Mifflin Company. All rights reserved.

Name _____

Choose a Topic

How do you choose a topic to write about?
You can choose a topic you already know about
or want to know about.

Write three topics you already know about.

1. _____

2. _____

3. _____

Choose one of these topics and write it inside the box in the middle. Then write something you know about this topic in each of the other four boxes.

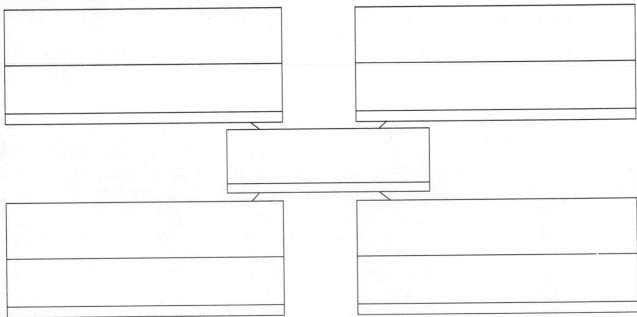

Write a sentence that tells what your paragraph will be about.

_____

Copyright © Houghton Mifflin Company. All rights reserved.

Name _____

Adding Details

This park ranger needs your help. Add details to his invitation to make it more interesting. The birds show where to add details. Write the new invitation below.

There are many things to see in the park!

In the ⟨bird⟩ pond, there are ⟨bird⟩ ducks

swimming. Many ⟨bird⟩ mushrooms grow

under the ⟨bird⟩ trees. Squirrels are getting

ready for a ⟨bird⟩ winter. Let me show you

around the park.

Come to the park!

_____

_____

_____

_____

_____

_____

Copyright © Houghton Mifflin Company. All rights reserved.

Name _____

A Funny Game

**Answer each pair of clues using
the words from the boxes.**

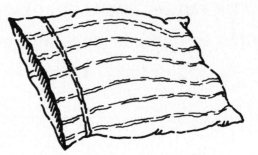

1. You rest your head on it. _____

   Someone who flies a jet _____

   | pilot   pillow |

2. Play time at school _____

   It flies up into the sky. _____

   | recess   rocket |

3. Very quick _____

   You use it on a shirt. _____

   | button   sudden |

4. Twelve eggs _____

   A bird with a red chest _____

   | robin   dozen |

5. Very quiet _____

   A dark place _____

   | silent   tunnel |

Copyright © Houghton Mifflin Company. All rights reserved.

Name _____

What a Great Day!

Read the story below. Use the words in the box to finish the story. You will use each word two times.

Word Bank

| across | brother | great | stand |

My _____ and I went to the

pond. We walked _____ the

bridge. I asked him to _____

next to a tall pine tree. I took his picture. My

_____ looked small next to that

_____ big tree. He could not

_____ still for very long. When

we looked _____ the pond, we

saw our father. He was bringing us lunch. He

gave us some _____ sandwiches.

We had fun together at the pond.

Copyright © Houghton Mifflin Company. All rights reserved.

Name _____

What's the Word?

Take a trip to the pond. Use words from the box to answer each question.

Word Bank

bank   crater   edge   moss   path   shallow

1. What do you follow to get to the pond?

   _____

2. What do you call the line where the water

   begins or ends? _____

3. What might you see growing under a tree?

   _____

4. What must you climb down to get to the

   pond? _____

5. What is another name for a hole in the

   ground? _____

6. What word describes water that is not

   very deep? _____

Copyright © Houghton Mifflin Company. All rights reserved.

Copyright © Houghton Mifflin Company. All rights reserved.

Name _____

Around the Pond Chart

As you read the story, complete the chart below by writing other categories of animals that Cammy and William found at the pond.

Birds	

Name _____

Follow the Clues!

Finish the chart. Write either the clues or the names of the animals that Cammy and William found at the pond.

Clue	Animal
1. white feathers stuck to bark	_____
2. _____ _____	raccoon
3. _____ _____	beaver
4. crater on sandy bottom of water	_____
5. _____	garter snake
6. _____	great blue heron
7. pile of mussel shells in mud	_____

Copyright © Houghton Mifflin Company. All rights reserved.

Name _____

Categorize and Classify

Read the story below. Complete the chart on page 114.

Around the Swamp

Wanda likes to visit the swamp. A swamp is a place that is very wet. Wanda's dad takes her around the swamp in his boat. They float under willow trees and gum trees.

Many animals live in the swamp. Wanda looks out for cottonmouth snakes. She knows they are very dangerous. Wanda's dad likes to watch for birds. He points out the hawks and vultures in the sky. There are many animals in the swamp that they never see. The fox only comes out at night, and the bobcat stays away from people. There is bass in the water, but the water is too dark to see the fish.

From the boat, Wanda can see turtles. The turtles lie in the sun and hardly move. Once they saw a raccoon catching a fish. But the most exciting day at the swamp was when they saw two black bear cubs running between the trees.

Copyright © Houghton Mifflin Company. All rights reserved.

Name _____

Categorize and Classify
(continued)

After you've read the story, complete the chart below.

At the bottom of the chart, make up your own category

about the swamp. Write some examples.

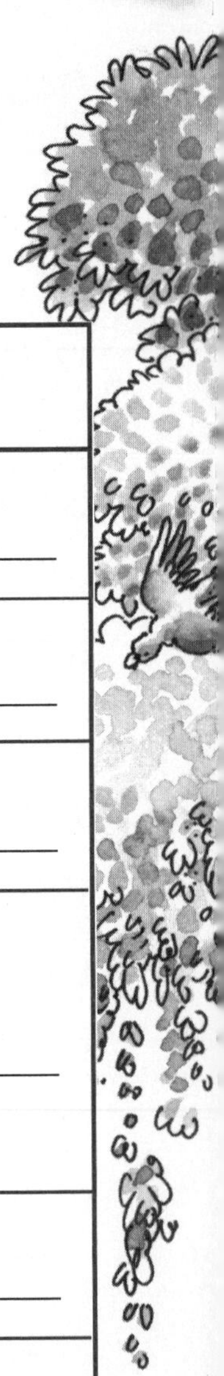

Category	Examples
Trees	_____
Snake	_____
Birds	_____
An Animal That Comes out at Night	_____
Fish	_____
An Animal That Eats Fish	_____
	_____
	_____

Copyright © Houghton Mifflin Company. All rights reserved.

Name _____

Blend the Sounds

Word Bank

| trip | stop | planting | fly | dry | sniff |

Write each word in the box under the picture whose
name begins with the same sound. Then write two other
words that begin with the same sound.

1. _____

2. _____

3. _____

4. _____

5. _____

6. _____

7. _____

8. _____

9. _____

10. _____

11. _____

12. _____

13. _____

14. _____

15. _____

16. _____

17. _____

18. _____

Copyright © Houghton Mifflin Company. All rights reserved.

Name _____

Double Consonants

In words like **bell**, **off**, and **dress**, the final
consonant sound is spelled with two letters
that are the same.

**Write the Spelling Words that end with the same
double consonant as *ball*.**

Spelling Words

1. bell
2. off
3. all
4. mess
5. add
6. hill
7. well
8. egg
9. will
10. grass

1. _____

2. _____

3. _____

4. _____

5. _____

**Write the Spelling Words that end with the same
double consonant as *dress*.**

6. _____

7. _____

Write the three Spelling Words that remain.

8. _____

9. _____

10. _____

Copyright © Houghton Mifflin Company. All rights reserved.

Copyright © Houghton Mifflin Company. All rights reserved.

Name _____

Spelling Spree

Write the Spelling Word that answers each riddle.

You can hear me ring.
What am I?

_____

You must clean me up.
What am I?

_____

If you drop me, my shell will break.
What am I?

_____

Climb up me. Roll back down.
What am I?

_____

Water me to keep me green.
What am I?

_____

Use a bucket to get my water.
What am I?

_____

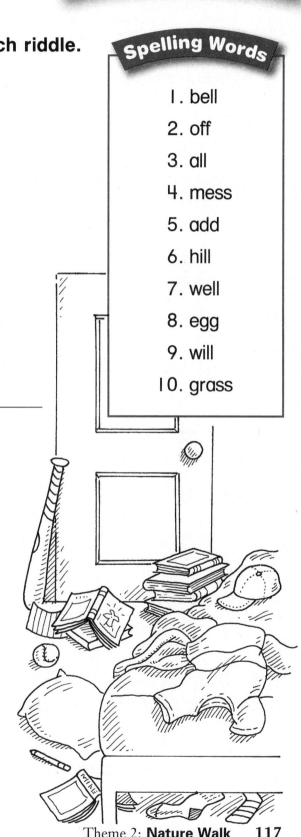

Spelling Words

1. bell
2. off
3. all
4. mess
5. add
6. hill
7. well
8. egg
9. will
10. grass

Theme 2: **Nature Walk**   117

Name _____

Proofreading and Writing

Proofreading Circle four Spelling Words that are spelled wrong. Then write each word correctly.

Spelling Words

1. bell
2. off
3. all
4. mess
5. add
6. hill
7. well
8. egg
9. will
10. grass

Dear Grandma,

   Today I walked to the pond with three friends. We alll sang as we walked. We passed some workers. They were deciding on where to ad more paths to the pond. We had fun watching a group of baby birds fly uff. We also saw a tiny blue egg in a nest. Soon a bird wil hatch from it!

   Love,

   Maria

1. _____

2. _____

3. _____

4. _____

Write a Letter On a separate piece of paper, write a letter to someone in your family. Tell them what you would like to see or do at the pond. Use Spelling Words from the list.

Copyright © Houghton Mifflin Company. All rights reserved.

Name _____

What Do You Mean?

**Read the two meanings for each word. Then write a
sentence for each meaning.**

Example: **can**

A **can** is something that soup comes in.

The word **can** means to be able to do something.

I will open the can.

Mary can read hard books.

watch: A **watch** is a small clock worn on the wrist.
To **watch** means to look at something.

1. _____

2. _____

tie: A **tie** is something men wear.
To **tie** means to fasten or close up something.

3. _____

4. _____

bark: Bark is what dogs do.
Bark is the covering on a tree.

5. _____

6. _____

Copyright © Houghton Mifflin Company. All rights reserved.

Theme 2: **Nature Walk**   119

Name _____

Excitement at the Pond

► A command is a sentence that tells someone to do something.

► An exclamation is a sentence that shows a strong feeling, such as surprise or fear.

Read each sentence. Write C if it is a command.
Write E if it is an exclamation.

_____ 1. Ming: I see a muskrat!

_____ 2. John: Let's take a picture of it!

_____ 3. Ming: Be very quiet.

_____ 4. John: Take a picture now.

Write each group of words as a command or an
exclamation. Use a capital letter and the correct end mark.

5. don't get close to the pond

_____

6. be careful where you step

_____

7. the water is cold

_____

Copyright © Houghton Mifflin Company. All rights reserved.

Name _____

Who's at the Pond?

**Under each picture write what Jenny is saying. Each
sentence should be an *exclamation*.**

1. _____   2. _____

_____   _____

**Pedro is at the pond with his mother. Look at the pictures.
Under each picture write what Pedro's mother says to him.
Each sentence should be a *command*.**

3. _____   4. _____

_____   _____

Copyright © Houghton Mifflin Company. All rights reserved.

Theme 2: **Nature Walk**   121

Name _____

It's a Field Trip!

**Read the announcement for the field trip to the pond.
Each sentence should be an exclamation or a command.
Check the capital letters and end marks for each
sentence. Circle any mistakes.**

> We're going on a field trip. plan to be gone
> all morning? bring a sweater! bring a snack?
> We're ready to have a good time.

**In the space below, write the announcement using
capital letters and end marks correctly.**

Copyright © Houghton Mifflin Company. All rights reserved.

Name _____

Learning Log

As you read the story, write a learning log entry for one of the pages in the story.

Notes About the Story	My Thoughts About My Notes
_____	_____
_____	_____
_____	_____
_____	_____
_____	_____
_____	_____
_____	_____
_____	_____
_____	_____
_____	_____

Copyright © Houghton Mifflin Company. All rights reserved.

Name _____

Tell More About the Story

Read the sentences in column A that tell about the story.

In column B, add more details to each sentence. Write your new

sentence on the line.

Story: Around the Pond	
A **Telling About the Story**	**B** **Adding More Details**
William and Cammy see white feathers.	_____ _____ _____
A tree has fallen.	_____ _____ _____
Cammy saw a shape on the tree.	_____ _____

Copyright © Houghton Mifflin Company. All rights reserved.

Name _____

Filling in the Blank

Use what you have learned about taking tests to help you complete fill-in-the-blank sentences with the correct answer. This practice will help you when you take this kind of test.

Read the sentence. Fill in the circle next to the answer that best completes the sentence.

1 Henry's mother knew more about _____ than his father.

○ singing   ○ camping

○ bears   ○ waterfalls

2 Both Henry and Mudge _____.

○ saw a fish jump out of a stream

○ smelled a deer

○ ate an oatmeal cookie

○ loved to go camping

3 Everyone in Henry's family had a _____, even Mudge.

○ cookie   ○ lantern

○ backpack   ○ tent

Copyright © Houghton Mifflin Company. All rights reserved.

Name _____

Filling in the Blank continued

4 Henry did not like it when his father _____.

- ○ sang love songs
- ○ cooked camp food
- ○ set up the tent
- ○ built the campfire

5 At night, Henry and his parents looked at the _____ in the sky.

- ○ rainbow
- ○ clouds
- ○ birds
- ○ stars

6 Inside the tent, Henry and Mudge _____ just like Henry's parents.

- ○ got ready to hike
- ○ snuggled
- ○ giggled
- ○ sang love songs

Copyright © Houghton Mifflin Company. All rights reserved.

Spelling Review

Write Spelling Words from the list to answer the questions.

1–7. Which words have the long **a**, **e**, **o**, or **u** sound spelled vowel-consonant-e?

1. _____   5. _____

2. _____   6. _____

3. _____   7. _____

4. _____

8–15. Which words have the consonant cluster **tr**, **sw**, **st**, **cl**, **br**, **gl**, or **xt**?

8. _____   12. _____

9. _____   13. _____

10. _____   14. _____

11. _____   15. _____

16–22. Which words have double consonants?

16. _____   20. _____

17. _____   21. _____

18. _____   22. _____

19. _____

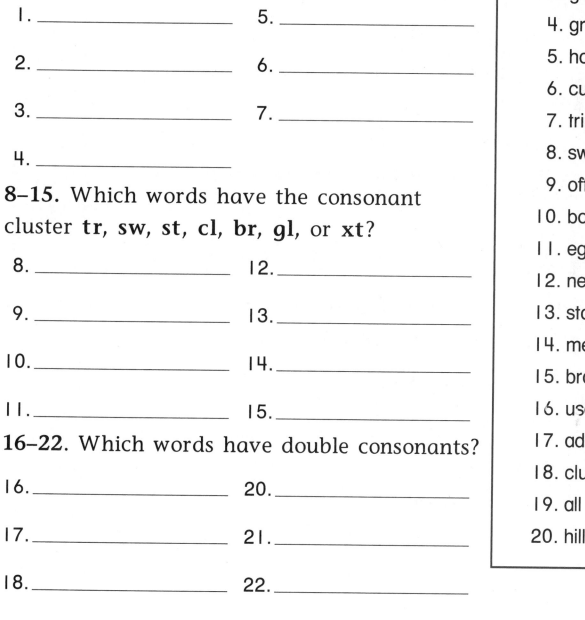

Spelling Words

1. lost
2. these
3. glad
4. grass
5. hope
6. cute
7. trip
8. swim
9. off
10. bone
11. egg
12. next
13. stone
14. mess
15. brave
16. use
17. add
18. club
19. all
20. hill

Copyright © Houghton Mifflin Company. All rights reserved.

Name _____

Spelling Spree

Double Delights Write the Spelling Word that answers each question.

Spelling Words

1. What can you hike up? _____

2. What grows in yards? _____

3. What does a chicken lay? _____

4. What is the opposite of **none**?

_____

Riddles Write a Spelling Word to answer each riddle.

5. This is something a dog likes. What is

this? _____

6. You do this in the water. What is this? _____

7. This is a group you join. What is this? _____

8. You can use this to build. What is this? _____

9. You can do this with numbers. What is this?

_____

10. If you are happy, you feel this way. What is this?

_____

Spelling Words

1. bone
2. hill
3. egg
4. swim
5. grass
6. all
7. stone
8. glad
9. club
10. add

Copyright © Houghton Mifflin Company. All rights reserved.

Name _____

Proofreading and Writing

Proofreading **Circle four Spelling Words that are wrong below. Then write each word correctly.**

Dear Gran,

Yesterday I went on a tripp to the lake with Mom. We saw cyute fish!

I have to go clean my room now. It is a mes! I hoap you will write back soon.

Love,
Celia

Spelling Words

1. brave
2. lost
3. cute
4. use
5. next
6. mess
7. off
8. these
9. hope
10. trip

1. _____   3. _____

2. _____   4. _____

Word for Word **Write the Spelling Word that means the opposite of each word or words.**

5. scared _____   7. waste _____   9. on _____

6. found _____   8. before _____   10. those _____

✏️ **Write a Story** **Write a story about a family on a nature walk. Write on another sheet of paper. Use the Spelling Review Words.**

Copyright © Houghton Mifflin Company. All rights reserved.

Name _____

Comparing Fables

Use the chart below to compare the five fables.

	Characters	**Main Event**	**Moral, or Lesson**
The Hare and the Tortoise			
The Crow and the Pitcher			
The Grasshopper and the Ants			
Belling the Cat			
The Fly on the Wagon			

Tell which fable was your favorite and why you liked it.

My favorite fable is _____.

I like it because _____

_____.

Copyright © Houghton Mifflin Company. All rights reserved.

Name _____

A Fable Character

An animal in a fable learns this lesson: *You do not make friends by being greedy.* How do you think the animal acts at the beginning of the fable? What does it think and say? Write some sentences about the animal who learns that lesson.

_____

_____

_____

_____

_____

Now draw a picture of the animal.

Copyright © Houghton Mifflin Company. All rights reserved.

Name _____

My Community

Describe your neighborhood or community. What does it look like? What do people like to do there? What do you like best about your neighborhood or community?

_____

_____

_____

_____

_____

_____

_____

Describe a place in your neighborhood or community that is important to you.

_____

_____

_____

Copyright © Houghton Mifflin Company. All rights reserved.

Name _____

Around Town: Neighborhood and Community

Fill in the chart as you read the stories.

	What neighborhood or community places appear in this theme?	Who are some of the community helpers in this theme?
Chinatown		
A Trip to the Firehouse		
Big Bushy Mustache		
Jamaica Louise James		

Copyright © Houghton Mifflin Company. All rights reserved.

Name _____

Which Word?

Circle the word that names or describes each picture.

Then use the circled word in a sentence.

1. watch   wash

_____

2. lunch   bathtub

_____

3. chain   path

_____

4. whispering   toothbrush

_____

5. gather   shopper

_____

Copyright © Houghton Mifflin Company. All rights reserved.

Name _____

Big, Bigger, or Biggest?

The word under the picture is a base word. On the line
under the middle box, add **-er** to the base word. On the
line under the last box, add **-est** to the base word. Then
draw pictures in the boxes to show the differences in size.

Example:

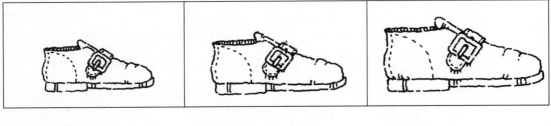

large _____   larger _____   largest _____

1.

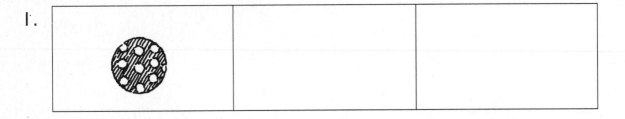

big _____   _____   _____

2.

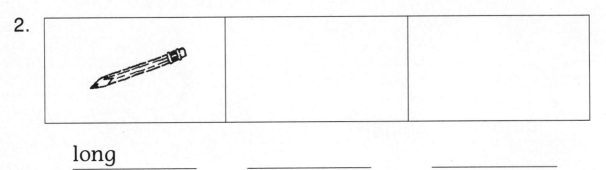

long _____   _____   _____

Copyright © Houghton Mifflin Company. All rights reserved.

Name _____

Matching and Sorting Words

Draw a line from each word to its meaning.

1. during   the season after fall
2. heard   throughout a certain time
3. lion   a large wild cat
4. winter   took in sounds with the ears

Word Bank

| during | heard | lion | winter |

Think how the words in each group are alike. Then choose one word from the box to add to each group of words below.

5. seen, smelled, _____

6. before, after, _____

7. summer, spring, _____

8. tiger, panther, _____

Use two of the words from the box in sentences.

9. _____

10. _____

Copyright © Houghton Mifflin Company. All rights reserved.

Name _____

Words to Draw

Draw a picture of someone making a delivery at an apartment. Then use each vocabulary word, *delivery* and *apartment*, in a sentence.

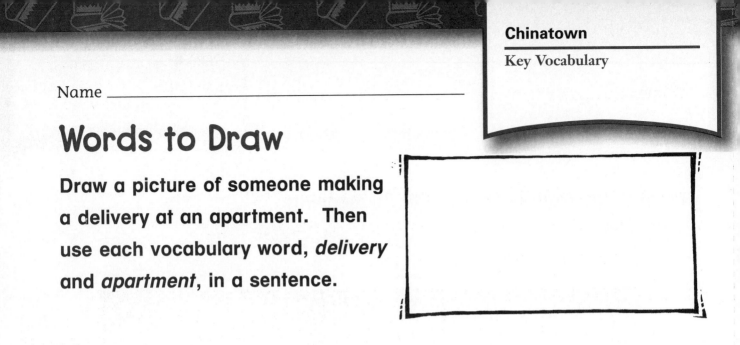

1. _____

2. _____

Draw a picture of people using handcarts at a market. Then use each vocabulary word, *handcarts* and *market*, in a sentence.

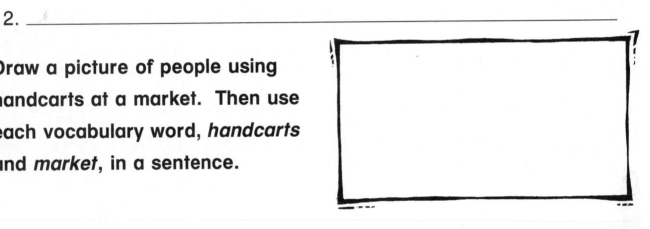

3. _____

4. _____

Draw a picture of a celebration. Then use the vocabulary word *celebration* in a sentence.

5. _____

Copyright © Houghton Mifflin Company. All rights reserved.

Name _____

What I Like Chart

As you read the story, choose pages that show
things you like to see in Chinatown. Write the page
number and a sentence next to it.

What I Like to See in Chinatown

page _____	
page _____	
page _____	
page _____	
page _____	
page _____	
page _____	
page _____	

Copyright © Houghton Mifflin Company. All rights reserved.

Name _____

Retelling the Story

Finish each sentence about Chinatown.

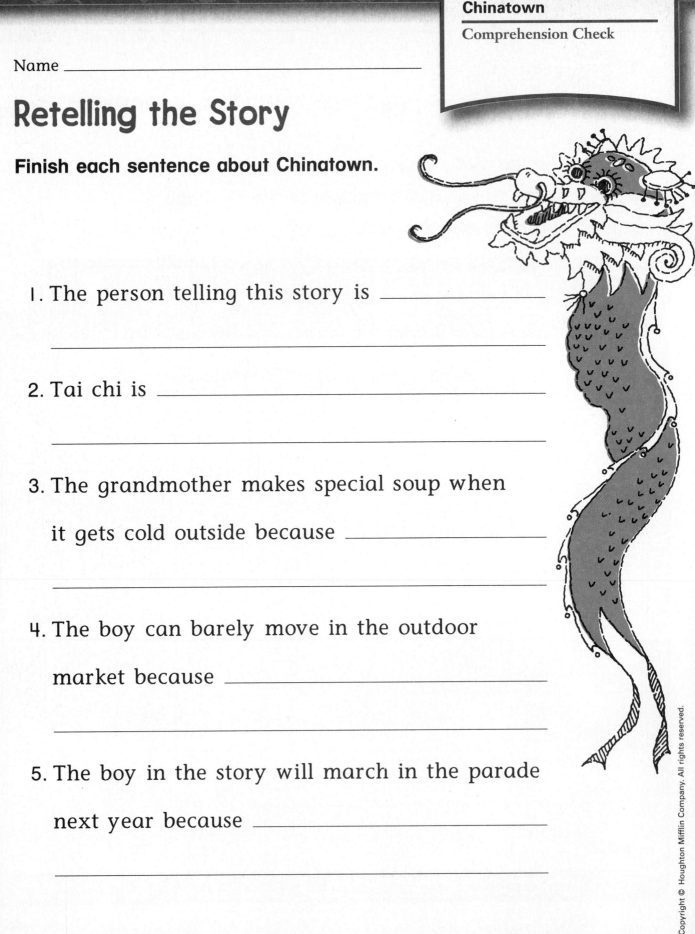

1. The person telling this story is _____

   _____

2. Tai chi is _____

   _____

3. The grandmother makes special soup when

   it gets cold outside because _____

   _____

4. The boy can barely move in the outdoor

   market because _____

   _____

5. The boy in the story will march in the parade

   next year because _____

   _____

Copyright © Houghton Mifflin Company. All rights reserved.

Name _____

Making Judgments

Read the story below.

Cowhands

Hank and Charlie are cowhands on a small cattle ranch. Their job is to herd the cows to town to be sold. This means that they must keep the cattle moving in the right direction. They do this by riding their horses beside the herd.

It is a long, dusty ride on the trails to town. Sometimes the dust is very thick. Hank and Charlie wear scarves called bandannas over their noses and mouths to keep the dust out. No matter how dusty it gets, Hank and Charlie must keep track of every cow.

When the sun goes down, Hank and Charlie find a place to camp. The cattle rest for the night. Hank and Charlie cook their dinner over a campfire. A delicious smell fills the air. The two cowhands are tired after a day of hard work. They spread out their sleeping bags and lie down under the stars. The camp is quiet. After a while Hank and Charlie hear a coyote howling in the distance. They both fall asleep as the coyote sings its song.

Copyright © Houghton Mifflin Company. All rights reserved.

Name _____

Making Judgments continued

After you have read the story "Cowhands,"
complete the chart below.

I Would / Would Not Like Chart

Things the Characters Do	I Would/Would Not Like This	Reasons Why I Feel This Way
1. _____ _____	_____ _____	_____ _____
2. _____ _____	_____ _____	_____ _____
3. _____ _____	_____ _____	_____ _____
4. _____ _____	_____ _____	_____ _____
5. _____ _____	_____ _____	_____ _____

Copyright © Houghton Mifflin Company. All rights reserved.

Name _____

Double the Fun

Use the double consonants in the box to finish each word.
Then write the word on the line.

| ck | ff | ll | ss |

duck   cuff   ball   dress

1. sme____ _____

2. po____et _____

3. gra____ _____

4. waterfa____ _____

5. sna____ _____

6. ski____ _____

7. gla____ _____

8. sni____ing _____

9. cla____ _____

10. cli____ _____

Copyright © Houghton Mifflin Company. All rights reserved.

Name _____

Two Letters—One Sound

Each Spelling Word is spelled with **th**, **wh**, **sh**, or **ch**. Each pair of letters stand for one sound.

Spelling Words

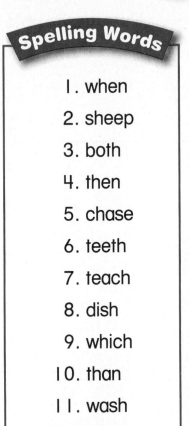

1. when
2. sheep
3. both
4. then
5. chase
6. teeth
7. teach
8. dish
9. which
10. than
11. wash
12. catch*

► the **th** sound ⟶ tha**t**, mo**th**er, smoo**th**
► the **wh** sound ⟶ **wh**y, some**wh**at
► the **sh** sound ⟶ **sh**e, friend**sh**ip, wi**sh**
► the **ch** sound ⟶ **ch**ild, sear**ch**ing, ri**ch**

Write each Spelling Word under the word with the same sound. The sound may be at the beginning, middle, or end of the word.

whale

chair

_____

_____

thumb

ship

_____

_____

_____

_____

_____

_____

_____

Copyright © Houghton Mifflin Company. All rights reserved.

Name _____

Spelling Spree

Word Fun Think how the words in each group are alike. Write the missing Spelling Words.

1. goats, horses, _____

2. rinse, scrub, _____

3. glass, fork, _____

4. lips, tongue, _____

5. throw, bounce, _____

6. learn, school, _____

Spelling Words

1. when
2. sheep
3. both
4. then
5. chase
6. teeth
7. teach
8. dish
9. which
10. than
11. wash
12. catch*

Write the two Spelling Words that rhyme with each other.

7. _____

8. _____

Copyright © Houghton Mifflin Company. All rights reserved.

Name _____

Proofreading and Writing

Proofreading Read the sentences below. Find and circle four Spelling Words that have spelling mistakes. Write them correctly.

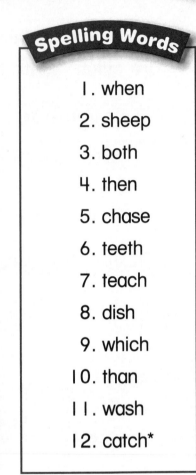

Spelling Words

1. Buth Grandma and I love to go to Chinatown.

2. We have a hard time deciding wich seafood restaurant we like best.

3. It is fun to watch the fish in the fish tank chace each other.

4. There is no fish fresher thun the fish in Chinatown.

Spelling Words

1. when
2. sheep
3. both
4. then
5. chase
6. teeth
7. teach
8. dish
9. which
10. than
11. wash
12. catch*

_____   _____

_____   _____

Writing Sentences On a separate sheet of paper, write four sentences that tell about a place you like to visit. Use Spelling Words from the list.

Copyright © Houghton Mifflin Company. All rights reserved.

Name _____

Knowing Your ABC's

Read the words in each box. Write the five words in ABC order.

Word Bank

| most | morning | move | mother | month |

1. _____   4. _____

2. _____   5. _____

3. _____

Word Bank

| restaurant | read | remember | report | rent |

6. _____   9. _____

7. _____   10. _____

8. _____

Copyright © Houghton Mifflin Company. All rights reserved.

Name _____

Who? What? Where?

All of the words in the box are naming words, or
nouns. Nouns name people, places, and things.

**Complete the chart below. Write words from the box to
show which nouns name people, places, and things.**

Word Bank

slide	city	boy	park	man
playground	swings	woman	monkey bars	girl

People

1. _____

2. _____

3. _____

4. _____

Places

5. _____

6. _____

7. _____

Things

8. _____

9. _____

10. _____

Copyright © Houghton Mifflin Company. All rights reserved.

Name _____

Spotlight on Naming Words

Naming words are called nouns. Nouns name
people, places, and things.

**Read each sentence. Underline the nouns that name
people. Circle the nouns that name things. Draw a box
around the nouns that name places.**

1. The baby is in the swing.

2. The pencil and paper
   belong to the student.

3. The family is at the beach.

4. The books are on the
   shelves in the library.

Copyright © Houghton Mifflin Company. All rights reserved.

Name _____

Revising a News Story

**Read the newspaper story. When possible, combine two
sentences into one to make the story sound better.**

Chinese New Year

Chinatown — Today was the Chinese New Year.
People who live in Chinatown celebrated. Visitors
celebrated. Adults crowded the streets. Children
crowded the streets. Boys from the kung fu school
marched down the streets. Girls from the kung fu
school marched down the streets. The dragon parade
was exciting to watch. The lion dance was exciting to
watch. The dragon costumes were beautiful. The lion
costume was beautiful. Everyone had a good time.

_____

_____

_____

_____

_____

Copyright © Houghton Mifflin Company. All rights reserved.

Name _____

Organizing a Story Scene

Write your ideas for a story scene.

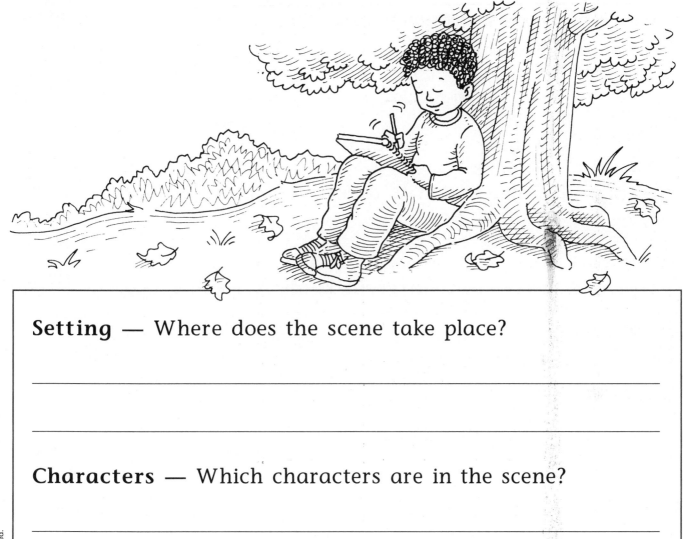

Setting — Where does the scene take place?

_____

_____

Characters — Which characters are in the scene?

_____

_____

Actions or Events — What happens in the scene?

_____

_____

Copyright © Houghton Mifflin Company. All rights reserved.

Name _____

To Be Exact

Write each sentence. Replace the underlined word with a more exact noun.

Example:

I visited my aunt at her **place**.

I visited my aunt at her **house**.

1. My aunt and I went to an outdoor <u>place</u> to buy

   food. _____

2. There were many different kinds of fresh <u>foods</u>

   there, such as apples and oranges. _____

   _____

3. My aunt bought three pounds of <u>fruit</u> to make a

   pie. _____

4. She paid the <u>person</u> for the fruit we bought.

   _____

5. When we got to my aunt's house, she made the pie

   and baked it in the <u>thing</u>. _____

   _____

Copyright © Houghton Mifflin Company. All rights reserved.

Name _____

Revising Your Friendly Letter

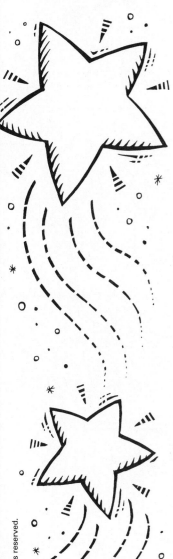

Superstar

☐ I included the five parts of a friendly letter.

☐ date   ☐ body   ☐ my name

☐ greeting   ☐ closing

☐ My topic is interesting to the reader.

☐ I used details in an interesting way.

☐ My letter shows something about me.

☐ I used different kinds of sentences.

Rising Star

☐ I included these parts of a friendly letter.

☐ date   ☐ body   ☐ my name

☐ greeting   ☐ closing

☐ I could add some details to tell more.

☐ My sentences are too much the same.

Copyright © Houghton Mifflin Company. All rights reserved.

Name _____

Different Kinds of Sentences

Read each sentence. Then write each sentence with the correct end mark.

1. I am very happy

   _____

2. Did you find my puppy

   _____

3. We went for a walk

   _____

4. This is a big surprise

   _____

Write a telling sentence about a dog.

_____

_____

Copyright © Houghton Mifflin Company. All rights reserved.

Name _____

Spelling Words

These Spelling Words are words that you use in your writing. Look carefully at how they are spelled. Write the missing letters in the Spelling Words below. Use the words in the box.

Spelling Words

1. n___m___   7. wh___t

2. o___   8. t_____

3. t_____e   9. d___

4. w_____t___   10. l___tt_____

5. m___s_____f   11. t___

6. w___nt   12. b_____n

Spelling Words

1. of
2. do
3. to
4. what
5. write
6. myself
7. name
8. time
9. went
10. been
11. too
12. little

Write the Spelling Words below.

_____   _____

_____   _____

_____   _____

_____   _____

_____   _____

_____   _____

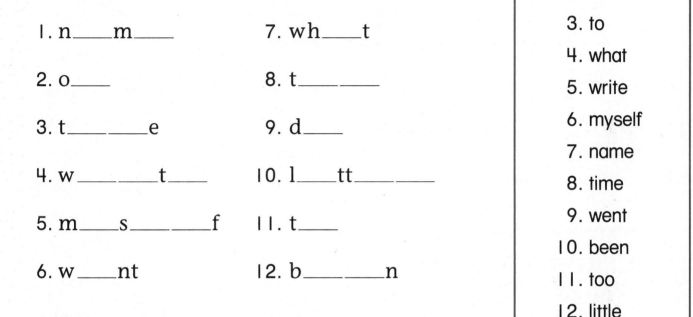

Copyright © Houghton Mifflin Company. All rights reserved.

Name _____

Spelling Spree

Choose a Spelling Word to complete each sentence. Write the words in the puzzles.

Spelling Words

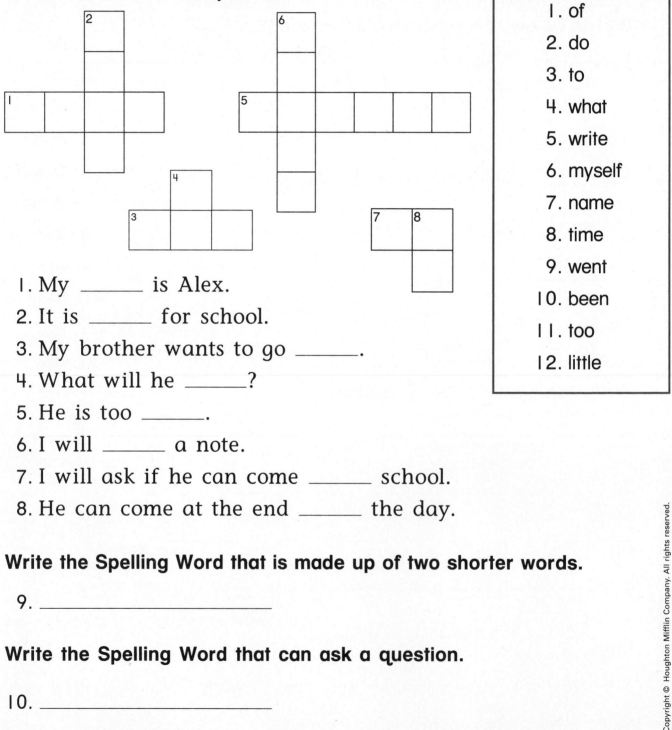

Spelling Words

1. of
2. do
3. to
4. what
5. write
6. myself
7. name
8. time
9. went
10. been
11. too
12. little

1. My _____ is Alex.

2. It is _____ for school.

3. My brother wants to go _____.

4. What will he _____?

5. He is too _____.

6. I will _____ a note.

7. I will ask if he can come _____ school.

8. He can come at the end _____ the day.

Write the Spelling Word that is made up of two shorter words.

9. _____

Write the Spelling Word that can ask a question.

10. _____

Copyright © Houghton Mifflin Company. All rights reserved.

Name _____

Proofreading and Writing

Proofreading Find and circle misspelled Spelling Words below. Then write each word correctly.

Copyright © Houghton Mifflin Company. All rights reserved.

October 5, 2001

Dear Akimi,

    It has not ben a good day. I whent to a new school. I did not know anyone in my class. I did not know whut to answer when the teacher asked me a question. I ate lunch by miself. In the afternoon I had to rite a story about my day.

Your friend,
Benita

Spelling Words

1. of
2. do
3. to
4. what
5. write
6. myself
7. name
8. time
9. went
10. been
11. too
12. little

1. _____ 4. _____

2. _____ 5. _____

3. _____

Write and Draw a Community Poster On construction paper, write the name of a community helper. Then write sentences that tell how that person helps. Use as many Spelling Words as you can.

Name _____

Train Play

Write the word that goes with each sentence.

Word Bank

| train | waited | spray | stay | day | paid |

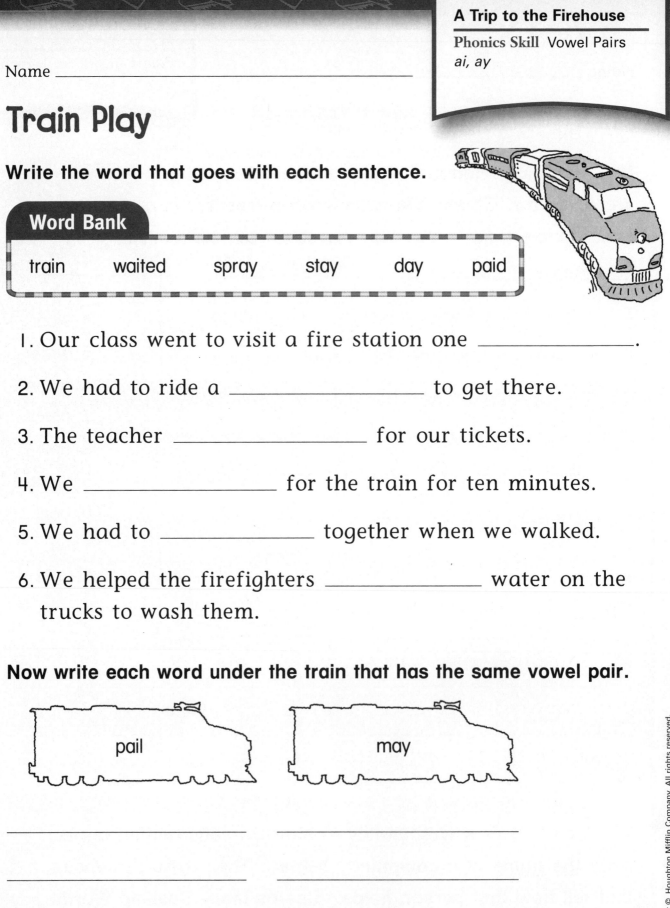

1. Our class went to visit a fire station one _____.

2. We had to ride a _____ to get there.

3. The teacher _____ for our tickets.

4. We _____ for the train for ten minutes.

5. We had to _____ together when we walked.

6. We helped the firefighters _____ water on the trucks to wash them.

Now write each word under the train that has the same vowel pair.

pail

may

_____   _____

_____   _____

_____   _____

Copyright © Houghton Mifflin Company. All rights reserved.

Name _____

Compound Word Find

Underline the compound words in the letter. Then add three sentences. Use words in the box to make compound words. Use those words in your sentences.

Word Bank					
day	flash	body	light	some	every

Dear Grandmother,

   Our new neighbor is a firefighter. Her

name is Ms. Sanchez.

   She let me visit the fire station yesterday.

I took my notebook so I could take lots of notes.

Ms. Sanchez showed me the water truck, the

ambulance, and the ladder truck. They were

parked in the firehouse driveway.

_____

_____

_____

Copyright © Houghton Mifflin Company. All rights reserved.

Name _____

Word Clues

Write a word from the box to complete the sentences.

Word Bank

clothes   guess   order

Find out what job Cal wants to do when he grows up. Read the clues to find out. Write the answer on the last line.

1. He wants to help people.

2. He will wear _____ that keep him safe from a fire. He will wear a big helmet, rubber boots, and a heavy coat.

3. He will drive a big truck.

4. He will help keep the buttons, knobs, and water hoses on his truck in working _____.

   Can you _____ what job Cal wants to do?

   wants to do? _____

Copyright © Houghton Mifflin Company. All rights reserved.

Name _____

Firefighter Words

Write a word or words from the box to tell what each sentence describes.

chief	gear	emergencies
firefighters	dispatch	fire engine

1. I am a truck with a siren and lights.

   _____

2. I tell the people what to do. _____

3. Air tanks and an ax can be very

   helpful. _____

4. We race to the fire and put it out.

   _____

5. Fires are burning and people need help.

   _____

6. When a message arrives, help is soon on

   the way. _____

Copyright © Houghton Mifflin Company. All rights reserved.

Name _____

Firehouse Chart

Complete the chart below as you read the story.

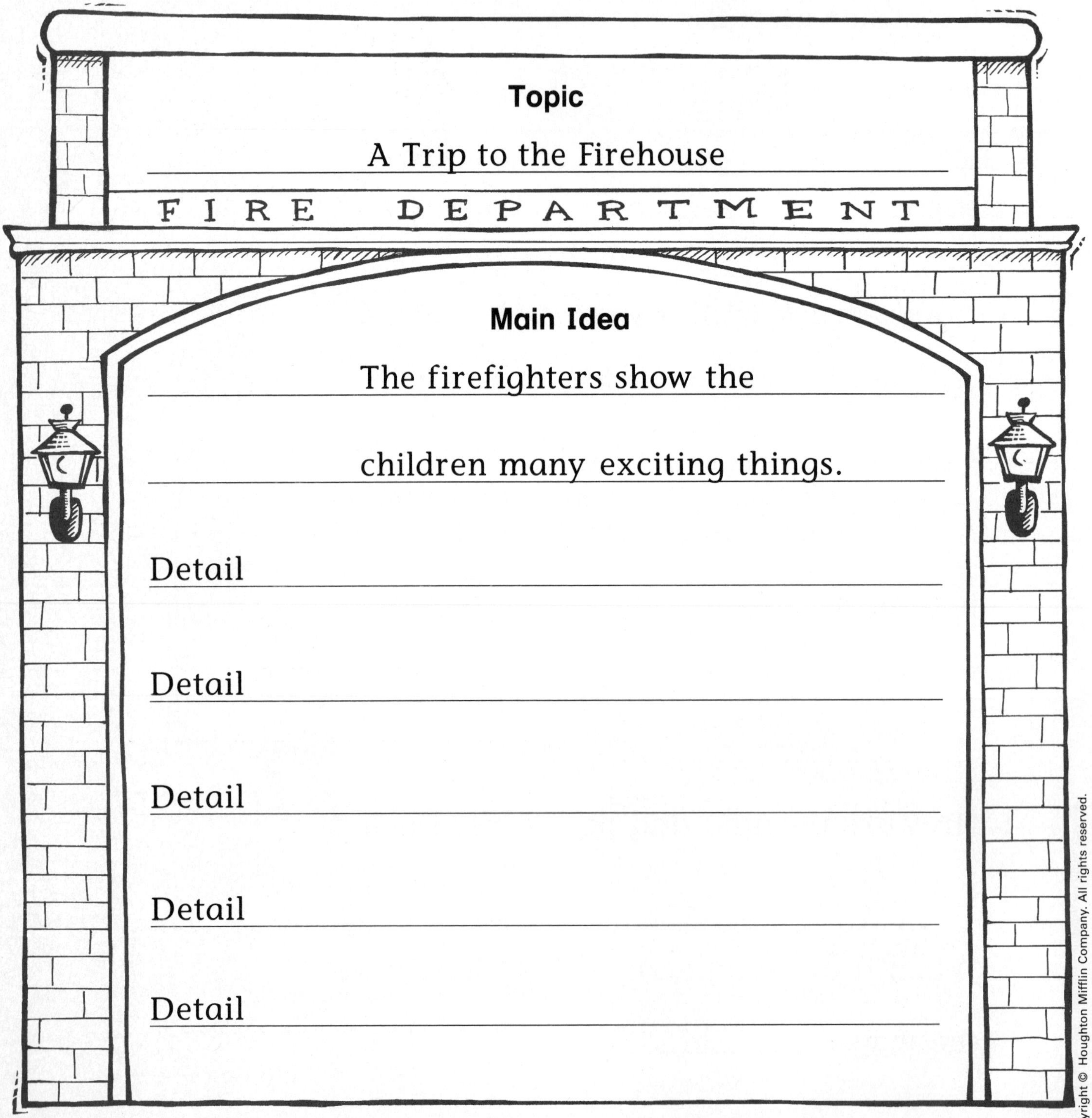

Topic

A Trip to the Firehouse

F I R E   D E P A R T M E N T

Main Idea

The firefighters show the

children many exciting things.

Detail _____

Detail _____

Detail _____

Detail _____

Detail _____

Copyright © Houghton Mifflin Company. All rights reserved.

Name _____

A Firefighter Is Talking

Pretend you are a firefighter. You are being asked questions on a TV show.

Write your answers on the lines.

1. What kind of gear do firefighters wear?

1. _____

_____

_____

2. Why is there a pole in a firehouse?

2. _____

_____

_____

3. What happens in the dispatch room in a firehouse?

3. _____

_____

_____

4. Why is it important to make sure all the equipment works?

4. _____

_____

_____

Copyright © Houghton Mifflin Company. All rights reserved.

Name _____

What's the Idea?

Read the newspaper story.

House Catches Fire

There was a fire in the kitchen of the Reese family home Thursday morning. The house is at 4301 Oak Line Drive. Two neighbors saw thick smoke coming through a window. One neighbor ran to her house to call 911. She told the emergency operator where the fire was. Another neighbor ran to the Reese house. She helped everyone in the family get out of the house safely.

The emergency operator called the fire station. A water truck and a fire engine were dispatched. The firefighters got to the Reese house within ten minutes. The firefighters hooked long hoses up to the water truck. They aimed the water at the fire. Soon, the fire was out. Everyone was safe because of the neighbors and the work of the firefighters.

The Reese family was happy that no one was hurt. The Reese family thanked the firefighters. They also thanked their neighbors.

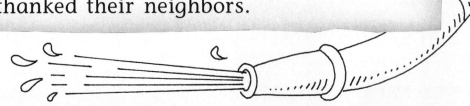

Copyright © Houghton Mifflin Company. All rights reserved.

Name _____

What's the Idea? continued

Use the newspaper story about the fire at the Reese home to complete the chart below.

Topic: _____

Main Idea: _____

_____

Detail 1: _____

_____

Detail 2: _____

_____

Detail 3: _____

_____

Detail 4: _____

_____

Copyright © Houghton Mifflin Company. All rights reserved.

Name _____

Consonant Choice

Write the word that completes each sentence.

1. Clang! Clang! The fire engine

   _____ down the street.

   | showed   rushed |

2. The firefighters wanted to

   _____ the fire in a hurry.

   | reach   chain |

3. The fire engine stopped at a plant

   _____.

   | ship   shop |

4. There was a fire burning in a

   _____.

   | wheelbarrow   whale |

5. Many people stopped to _____
   the firefighters work.

   | watch   check |

6. _____ quickly pulled out
   the water hoses.

   | Those   They |

7. The firefighters sprayed water

   _____.

   | when   everywhere |

8. The store owner _____ the
   firefighters before they left.

   | thought   thanked |

Copyright © Houghton Mifflin Company. All rights reserved.

166   Theme 3: **Neighborhood and Community**

Name _____

ai or *ay*?

Most of the words have the long **a** sound spelled **ay** or **ai**.

the long **a** sound ———→ **way, train**

▶ The word **they** is special. The vowels **ey** spell the long **a** sound in **they**.

▶ The word **great** is special. The vowels **ea** spell the long **a** sound in **great**.

Write each Spelling Word under the hat with the matching letters.

Spelling Words

1. train
2. way
3. mail
4. play
5. trail
6. pay
7. sail
8. hay
9. nail
10. rain
11. they*
12. great*

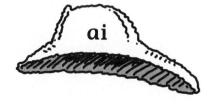 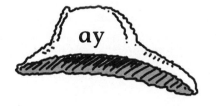

_____   _____

_____   _____

_____   _____

_____   _____

_____   _____

Write the special words that have a star next to them.

_____   _____

Copyright © Houghton Mifflin Company. All rights reserved.

Name _____

Spelling Spree

Maze Play Connect the words with the long *a* sound to help the fire truck get to the fire.

Spelling Words

1. train
2. way
3. mail
4. play
5. trail
6. pay
7. sail
8. hay
9. nail
10. rain
11. they*
12. great*

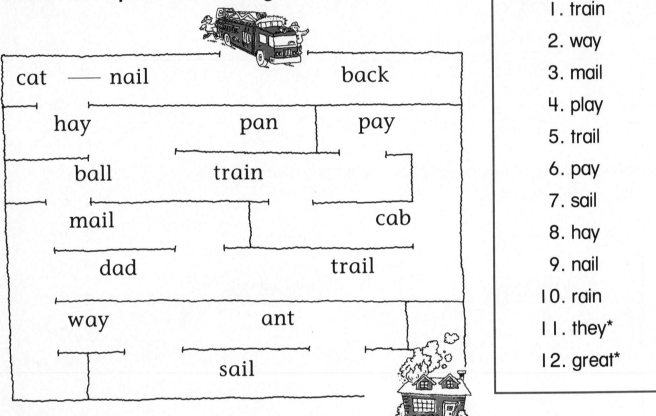

cat — nail   back

hay   pan   pay

ball   train

mail   cab

dad   trail

way   ant

sail

Write each Spelling Word in the maze under its long *a* spelling.

ai   ay

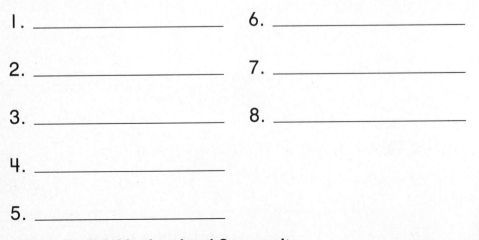

1. _____   6. _____

2. _____   7. _____

3. _____   8. _____

4. _____

5. _____

Copyright © Houghton Mifflin Company. All rights reserved.

Name _____

Proofreading and Writing

Proofreading Circle the four Spelling Words that are wrong in this letter. Then write each word correctly.

Copyright © Houghton Mifflin Company. All rights reserved.

> January 23, 2001
>
> Dear Chief Rogers,
>
> We had a grate time at the fire station! It was fun to pla with Spot, the firehouse dog. Everyone liked washing the fire truck too. The way the water came out of the hose looked like ran. I liked watching the firefighters get ready to go fight a fire. Thay dressed really fast. May I come visit another day?
>
> Sincerely,
> Tony

_____   _____

_____   _____

Spelling Words

1. train
2. way
3. mail
4. play
5. trail
6. pay
7. sail
8. hay
9. nail
10. rain
11. they*
12. great*

Write What You Want to See
What would you like to see if you could visit a firehouse? Write it on a separate sheet of paper. Use Spelling Words from the list.

Name _____

Dictionary Word Match

Read the word list. Write each word under the place where you would find it in the dictionary. Would the word be found in the beginning, middle, or end?

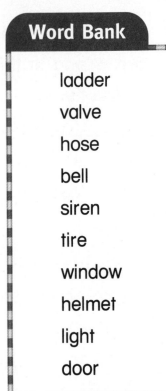

Word Bank

- ladder
- valve
- hose
- bell
- siren
- tire
- window
- helmet
- light
- door

Beginning
A–K

Middle
L–S

End
T–Z

_____   _____   _____

_____   _____   _____

_____   _____   _____

_____

Copyright © Houghton Mifflin Company. All rights reserved.

Name _____

Names of Nouns

► A special noun is a word that names a certain, or special, person, place, or thing.
► A special noun always begins with a capital letter.

Read each noun below. Write a special noun for it. Choose special nouns from the box.

Word Bank

Red River

Mrs. Carlos

Texas

Spot

Bay City

Playland Park

Golden Gate
  Bridge

Mr. R. Davis

1. park _____

2. woman _____

3. bridge _____

4. dog _____

5. state _____

6. river _____

7. city _____

8. man _____

Write two sentences about a place you like to visit. Use a special noun in each sentence.

_____

_____

_____

Copyright © Houghton Mifflin Company. All rights reserved.

Name _____

Name Those Facts

► A special noun is a word that names a certain, or special, person, place, or thing.

► A special noun always begins with a capital letter.

special person   special place   special thing

Complete each sentence with a special noun that tells about you.

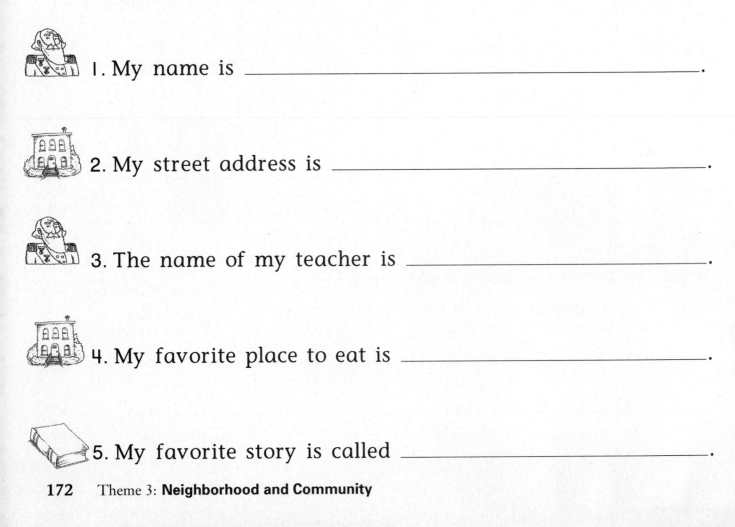

1. My name is _____.

2. My street address is _____.

3. The name of my teacher is _____.

4. My favorite place to eat is _____.

5. My favorite story is called _____.

172   Theme 3: **Neighborhood and Community**

Copyright © Houghton Mifflin Company. All rights reserved.

Name _____

Special Names

Replace the words in dark print with special names.
Write the names on the lines below.

May 29, 2001

Dear Joan,

   Today was a very exciting **day**. **My friend** and I were walking down **the street**. A fire truck came racing past us. It stopped at the house of **our neighbor**. We ran to see what was wrong. We found that **a cat** was stuck in a tree.

                                    Yours truly,
                                    Meg

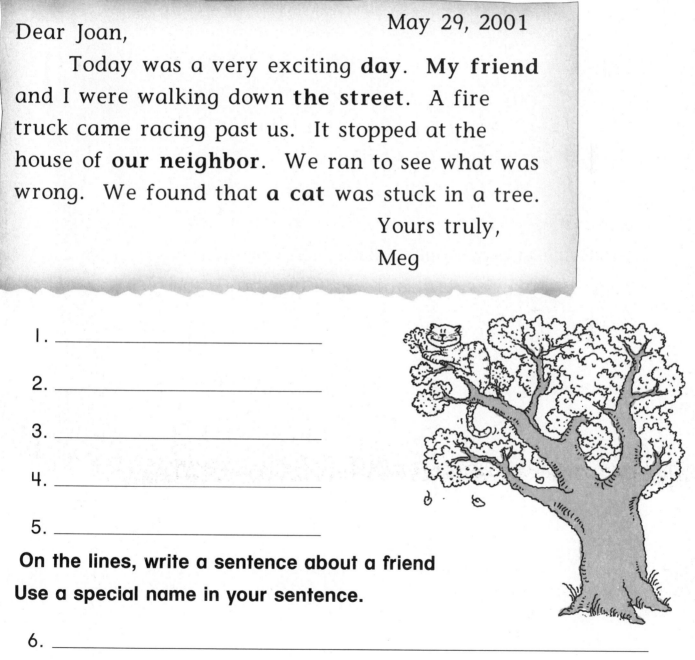

1. _____

2. _____

3. _____

4. _____

5. _____

On the lines, write a sentence about a friend
Use a special name in your sentence.

6. _____

_____

Copyright © Houghton Mifflin Company. All rights reserved.

Name _____

Web Notes

**Read the paragraph. Write your notes
about the paragraph in the web.**

Fire Safety Rules

Suppose you are in a building that catches
fire. First stay calm. Warn everyone in the
building about the fire. Be careful though, you
must get out quickly. Feel doors to see if they
are hot. If they are, the fire may be burning
on the other side. See if there is another way
out. Once you are out, call the firefighters.
Never go back inside a burning building.

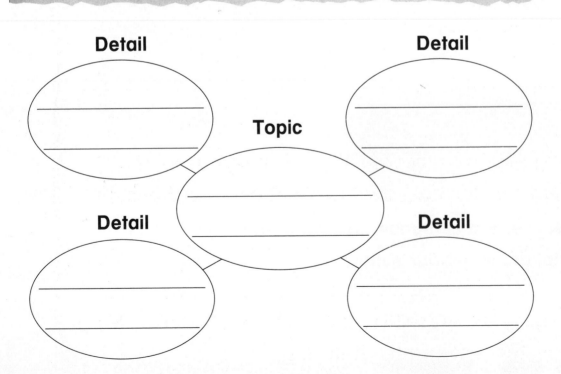

Detail

Detail

Topic

Detail

Detail

Copyright © Houghton Mifflin Company. All rights reserved.

Name _____

Making It Clear

**Read the dialogue. Then rewrite the Caller's answers.
Add special nouns that give exact information.**

Emergency Operator: 911 Operator.
Caller: There is a fire at a store.

_____

_____

Emergency Operator: What is the address?
Caller: The store is near a busy street.

_____

_____

Emergency Operator: What is your name?
Caller: Pam.

_____

_____

Emergency Operator: Where are you now?
Caller: I'm looking out the window of a house.

_____

_____

Emergency Operator: Stay where you are. Help
will be there in a few minutes.

Copyright © Houghton Mifflin Company. All rights reserved.

Name _____

Letter Magic

Change one letter in each word in dark print to make a new word that will finish each sentence. Each new word should have the letters *ow* or *ou* in it.

1. **cut**   He's not going in. He's going _____ .

2. **cot**   That's not a pig. That's a _____ .

3. **load**   She's not being quiet. She's being _____ .

4. **horse**   That's not a barn. That's a _____ .

5. **flowed** That's not a tree. That's a _____ .

6. **short**   Speak softly. Don't _____ .

Look at the words you wrote. Choose one word that has the letters *ou* and one word that has the letters *ow*. Write a sentence with each of those words.

7. _____

8. _____

Copyright © Houghton Mifflin Company. All rights reserved.

Name _____

Suffix Fun

Write the base word of each underlined word.

1. Sarah likes her <u>colorful</u> costume. _____

2. She feels <u>playful</u> when she puts it on. _____

3. On the stage, she has to sing <u>loudly</u>. _____

4. But at home she sings <u>quietly</u> to herself. _____

5. She had to learn her songs <u>quickly</u>. _____

6. She is <u>thankful</u> she has a good part in the play.

_____

Add -*ly* or -*ful* to the words below to make new words.

7. silent _____

8. skill _____

9. hope _____

10. sad _____

Copyright © Houghton Mifflin Company. All rights reserved.

Name _____

Use the Words

Word Bank

behind   soldier   story

Answer each riddle with a word from the box.

1. I have a beginning and an end. What am I? _____

2. I keep our country safe. Who am I? _____

3. I mean the opposite of "in front." _____

Write a short story about a soldier who sees
a horse behind a tree. Use all of the words
from the box in your story.

_____

_____

_____

_____

Copyright © Houghton Mifflin Company. All rights reserved.

Name _____

Costume Play

José is in the school play. Follow these directions to show how José will look.

Directions:

1. Draw the costume of a king on José. Include a crown.
2. Draw a bushy beard.
3. Draw a big mustache.

José and his mom are talking. Use the words in the box to complete their sentences.

> ### Vocabulary
>
> handsome   disguise   mirror

Mom: "What a _____ king we have here!"

José: "I'm not really a king. I'm wearing a _____."

Mom: "Then who are you?"

José: "I'm José, your son."

Mom: "You'd better look in a _____ to be sure!"

Copyright © Houghton Mifflin Company. All rights reserved.

Name _____

Problem-Solving Event Map

As you read the story, complete the Problem-Solving Event Map below.

Problem: Ricky loses the _____ his teacher gave him.

What Ricky Tries	Predict: Will this solve the problem?	Check: Does this work?
_____ _____ _____	Yes No	_____
_____ _____	Yes No	_____
_____ _____	Yes No	_____
_____ _____	Yes No	_____
_____ _____	Yes No	_____

Copyright © Houghton Mifflin Company. All rights reserved.

Name _____

True or Not True?

Print the word *True* or *Not true* after each sentence.

1. Ricky was happy that he looked like his mother. _____

2. Mrs. Cortez asked the children to leave their costumes in their desks. _____

3. Ricky looked older with his mustache on. _____

4. Ricky told his father all about the lost mustache. _____

5. Ricky tried to make his own mustache. _____

6. Ricky's father shaved his mustache so he would look more like Ricky. _____

7. Ricky's new mustache was a special gift from his father. _____

Find each sentence that was *Not true*. On the lines below, rewrite each sentence to make it true.

8. _____

9. _____

   _____

10. _____

   _____

Copyright © Houghton Mifflin Company. All rights reserved.

Name _____

Problem-Solving

Read the story. Then complete the chart on the next page.

The Cookie Problem

Mike's class wanted to do something special for the children at the hospital. They decided to raise money to buy books. They would have a cookie sale at school. Everyone would bring cookies to sell.

When he got home, Mike asked his mother for help making cookies. She reminded him that she had to go to work soon.

Mike asked his father for help. His father wanted to help, but he had promised to help Mike's sister build her science project.

Mike decided to count his money. He had been saving to buy a new model to build. He could buy cookies, but then he would have to wait even longer to get the model.

Then Mike had an idea. He called his friend Tran. They could make cookies together! Tran's grandfather would help them. Mike took sugar and flour to Tran's house. Mike and Tran and Tran's grandfather made cookies. The next day, the class sold cookies. They used the money to buy ten books for the children at the hospital.

Copyright © Houghton Mifflin Company. All rights reserved.

182   Theme 3: **Neighborhood and Community**

Name _____

Problem-Solving continued

After you've read the story "The Cookie Problem," answer this question.

What is Mike's problem?

_____

In the box on the left, write each solution Mike tries. In the box on the right, write why it doesn't work.

Solution	Why It Doesn't Work

Mike's last solution does work. Write the solution and why it works.

_____

_____

Do you think Mike's solution is a good one? Why or why not?

_____

Copyright © Houghton Mifflin Company. All rights reserved.

Name _____

Play Day

**Choose the word with *ai* or *ay* that correctly completes
each sentence. Write the word on the line.**

1. Ray has a part in the school _____. | play   jail |

2. He can't _____ to act on the stage. | stay   wait |

3. Ray has one of the _____ parts. | main   hay |

4. He has to _____ his lines many
   times to remember them. | main   say |

5. After the show is over, everyone will

   _____ Ray's hard work. | gray   praise |

6. _____ he will even be the star
   of the play! | faintly   maybe |

**Write two sentences of your own. Use an *ai* word in one
sentence and an *ay* word in the other.**

_____

_____

Copyright © Houghton Mifflin Company. All rights reserved.

Name _____

The Vowel Sound in cow

The words **town** and **house** have the same
vowel sound. This vowel sound may be
spelled **ow** or **ou**.   The words **could** and
should do not follow this rule.

**Write the Spelling Words with the *ow* sound
spelled *ow*.**

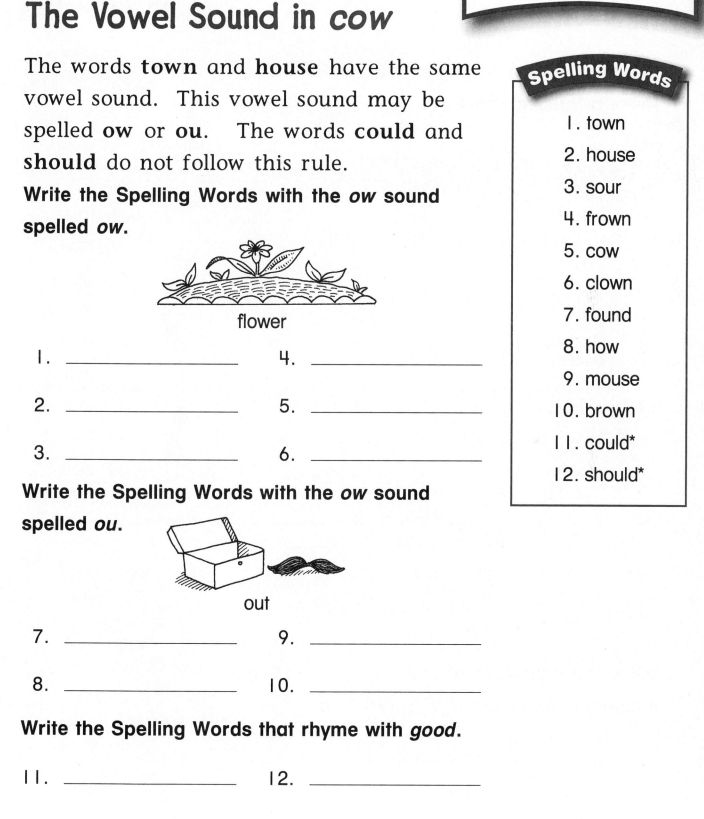

flower

1. _____   4. _____

2. _____   5. _____

3. _____   6. _____

**Write the Spelling Words with the *ow* sound
spelled *ou*.**

out

7. _____   9. _____

8. _____   10. _____

Write the Spelling Words that rhyme with *good*.

11. _____   12. _____

Copyright © Houghton Mifflin Company. All rights reserved.

Spelling Words

1. town
2. house
3. sour
4. frown
5. cow
6. clown
7. found
8. how
9. mouse
10. brown
11. could*
12. should*

Name _____

Spelling Spree

Spelling Scramble Unscramble the letters to
make a Spelling Word.

1. w n o r f ___ ___ ___ ___ ___

2. s d u o h l ___ ___ ___ ___ ___ ___

3. u s o h e ___ ___ ___ ___ ___

4. w o r n b ___ ___ ___ ___ ___

5. u o l d c ___ ___ ___ ___ ___

6. w n l c o ___ ___ ___ ___ ___

Spelling Words

1. town
2. house
3. sour
4. frown
5. cow
6. clown
7. found
8. how
9. mouse
10. brown
11. could*
12. should*

Fill-in Fun Write the missing Spelling Word to
create a pair of words that go together.

7. sweet and _____

8. lost and _____

9. _____ and country

10. cat and _____

Copyright © Houghton Mifflin Company. All rights reserved.

Proofreading and Writing

Proofreading Circle four Spelling Words that are spelled wrong in this note. Then write each word correctly.

Copyright © Houghton Mifflin Company. All rights reserved.

Dear Parents,

For the school play, could you help us with costumes? Here's what we need:

► A tail for the couw

► Big shoes for the cloun

► Broun pants and shirt for the mowse

Thank you for your help!

Mr. Jackson

Spelling Words

1. town
2. house
3. sour
4. frown
5. cow
6. clown
7. found
8. how
9. mouse
10. brown
11. could*
12. should*

1. _____   3. _____

2. _____   4. _____

Write a Letter Pretend you have just been in a play about Cinco de Mayo. On a separate piece of paper, write a letter to a friend. Tell about the play. Use Spelling Words from the list.

Name _____

Search for Meaning

Read each sentence. Use the context to figure out what the underlined word means. Write the letter for the meaning of the word on the line next to each sentence.

_____ 1. When our team scored the winning point, the fans cheered for our victory.

_____ 2. We celebrated by inviting all of our friends to eat cake and sing.

_____ 3. We rushed home so we could be the first ones there for the party.

_____ 4. Rosie lost her hat, so she retraced her steps and looked everywhere she had been.

_____ 5. My mother's special creation for the party was a drink she made from ice cream, pineapple, and bananas.

Meanings

A. went back over

B. win or getting first place

C. something made up

D. had a party for a special reason

E. went quickly

Copyright © Houghton Mifflin Company. All rights reserved.

Name _____

Which Is Which?

▶ Nouns can name one thing or more than one thing.

▶ Most nouns add -**s** to name more than one.

▶ Nouns that end in **s**, **x**, **ch**, and **sh** add -**es** to name more than one.

Look at the nouns in the box. Some name one thing and some name more than one thing. Write the nouns that name one thing below the flag. Write the nouns that name more than one thing below the group of flags.

Word Bank

| boxes | shoes | dishes | dresses | mustache |
| pocket | apples | wish | fox | father |

_____   _____

_____   _____

_____   _____

_____   _____

Copyright © Houghton Mifflin Company. All rights reserved.

Name _____

What Do You See?

Remember:

► Nouns can name one thing or more than one thing.

► Most nouns add **-s** to name more than one.

► Nouns that end in **s**, **x**, **ch**, and **sh** add **-es** to name more than one.

Write what you see in each spot. The first one has been done for you.

apple

I see <u>two apples</u>

_____ .

mustache

I see _____

_____ .

dress

I see _____

_____ .

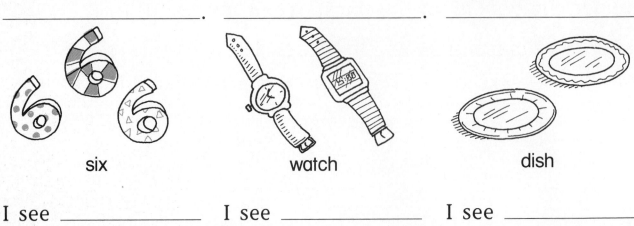

six

I see _____

_____ .

watch

I see _____

_____ .

dish

I see _____

_____ .

Copyright © Houghton Mifflin Company. All rights reserved.

Name _____

Where's That Mustache?

Remember:

► Nouns can name one thing or more than
one thing.

► Most nouns add **-s** to name more than one.

► Nouns that end in **s**, **x**, **ch**, and **sh** add **-es**
to name more than one.

**Suppose Ricky wrote a report about his lost mustache.
He made five mistakes in his report. Circle his
mistakes. Then write each word correctly.**

I lost my mustache. I looked everywhere for
it. I looked in my pocketes. I looked in the boxs
in my closet. I looked under the dishs. I looked
under the chaires in the kitchen. I even looked
under the benchs in the park. Then my mother
surprised me with a new mustache!

1. _____   4. _____

2. _____   5. _____

3. _____

Copyright © Houghton Mifflin Company. All rights reserved.

Name _____

What Is the Problem?

Think of a problem that you have had. How did you solve it? What did you learn from the problem and the solution? Use this chart to help you organize your ideas about the problem.

1. What was the problem? How did it come up?

_____

_____

2. How did you solve the problem?

_____

_____

3. What did you learn from solving the problem?

_____

_____

Copyright © Houghton Mifflin Company. All rights reserved.

Name _____

Solving a Problem

**Read the school newspaper report. It tells about a play
put on by the second grade. Make the writing more
interesting by replacing the underlined words with
exact nouns. Write your choices for exact nouns on
the lines below.**

Last night, the second grade put on a play.
The teacher said it was about Cinco de Mayo.
Two children played instruments. One girl told
the story. All the students wore costumes. Boys
wore sombreros and carried things. Girls wore
skirts and serapes. When the play ended,
everyone clapped.

1. _____

2. _____

3. _____

4. _____

5. _____

Copyright © Houghton Mifflin Company. All rights reserved.

Name _____

Rhyme Time

Here are some poems about painting. Finish each poem. Write a word from the box that rhymes with the last word in the first sentence.

Word Bank

dream	easy	sea	street	week

1. The beach is a place where I like to be.

   That's where I go when I paint the _____.

2. Things are not always what they seem.

   Today I'll paint a funny _____.

3. Here's a painting of a dog with furry feet.

   He's walking down a busy _____.

4. How can I paint on a day that's breezy?

   That's a job that won't be _____!

5. At this painting you may not peek.

   You will have to wait a _____.

Copyright © Houghton Mifflin Company. All rights reserved.

Name _____

What Do You See?

Choose a word from the box to label each picture.

Copyright © Houghton Mifflin Company. All rights reserved.

Word Bank

celebration   furniture   lotion   nature   picture   vacation

_____

_____

_____

_____

_____

_____

Name _____

I Believe in Art

The Lady with the Flowers

Grammy Spends the Whole Evening Sewing

I Can't Believe I Ate the Whole Thing!

Write the name of the painting to answer each question.

1. Which painting shows someone with a needle and thread?

_____

2. Which painting shows someone sitting in front of an empty plate?

_____

3. Which painting shows someone carrying roses?

_____

Make your own drawing called *I Believe in Happiness*.

I Believe in Happiness

Copyright © Houghton Mifflin Company. All rights reserved.

Name _____

Subway Words

Maria is new to the city. She asks her friend Lulu how to get around. Finish the sentences with words from the box.

Vocabulary

booth   plaque   station   subway   token

Maria: How can I get around in the city?

Lulu: You can use the _____.

Maria: Where can I go to find it?

Lulu: You will find a _____ close to your house.

Maria: Then what do I do?

Lulu: You go down the stairs and find a _____ where you buy a _____. Then you get on the train.

Maria: How do I know where to get off?

Lulu: When the train slows down, look out the window. You will see a _____ with the name of the station on it.

Copyright © Houghton Mifflin Company. All rights reserved.

Name _____

I Can Use Clues Chart

As you read, use clues from the story to make guesses
about what Jamaica and the other people in the story
are like. Write your guesses and the clues on the chart.

Story: Jamaica Louise James	
What the Character Is Like	**Story Clues**
_____	_____
_____	_____
_____	_____
_____	_____
_____	_____
_____	_____
_____	_____
_____	_____

Copyright © Houghton Mifflin Company. All rights reserved.

Name _____

How Does It Feel?

Read each sentence. Choose the word that best completes the sentence. Write the word on the line.

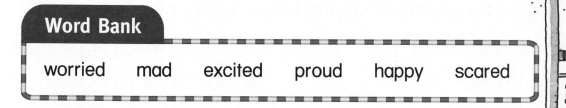

Word Bank

worried   mad   excited   proud   happy   scared

1. Grammy and Mama are _____ about their birthday present for Jamaica. They want her to open it quickly.

2. Jamaica is _____ about how much the present cost.

3. Grammy is not _____ to work at night, but Jamaica is afraid of the night.

4. The grown-ups in the subway always look so _____.

5. Grammy is very _____ when she sees Jamaica's paintings.

6. Now the people in the subway seem _____. They like Jamaica's presents.

Copyright © Houghton Mifflin Company. All rights reserved.

Name _____

Making Inferences

Read the story. Then answer the questions on page 201.

Luann's House

Luann lives with her Aunt Sonya and Uncle Leo on the top floor of their building. Luann's best friend lives next door. Her name is Carla.

Luann has three pets. She has a gerbil in a small cage, a parrot in a big cage, and a cat that likes to go on the roof. Luann gives her gerbil balls of cotton to make into nests. She feeds the parrot pieces of fruit and slices of bread. When Luann and Carla go up to the roof, Luann brings her cat.

Uncle Leo reads in a big chair with a light behind it. Sometimes he reads to Carla and Luann about the new paintings at the museum.

Aunt Sonya has a garden on the roof. She grows roses. She knows the names of all the roses. Sometimes she brings fresh bread and iced tea up to the roof for the girls.

Copyright © Houghton Mifflin Company. All rights reserved.

200   Theme 3: **Neighborhood and Community**

Name _____

Making Inferences continued

Use the things you know about Luann from the story to answer the questions. Do the same with Uncle Leo and Aunt Sonya.

1. What is special about Luann?

   _____

   _____

   _____

Luann

2. What kind of person is Uncle Leo?

   _____

   _____

   _____

Uncle Leo

3. Would you like Aunt Sonya to take care of you for an afternoon? Why?

   _____

   _____

   _____

Aunt Sonya

Copyright © Houghton Mifflin Company. All rights reserved.

Name _____

Riddle Fun

Find two words from the box that go together to match each description.

Word Bank			
clown	cow	growling	frowning
house	mouse	loud	prowling

1. A place where there is lots of noise

_____

2. A small animal sneaking around

_____

3. A funny guy at the circus who is unhappy

_____

4. An angry animal that gives milk

_____

Copyright © Houghton Mifflin Company. All rights reserved.

Name _____

E? Ea? Ee?

The vowel sound in **we**, **keep**, and **clean** is the long **e** sound. The long **e** sound may be spelled **e**, **ee**, or **ea**.

► The words **people** and **the** do not follow this pattern.

Spelling Words

1. clean
2. keep
3. please
4. feel
5. we
6. be
7. eat
8. tree
9. mean
10. read
11. the*
12. people*

Write the Spelling Words with the long *e* sound spelled *e*.

_____ _____

Write the Spelling Words with the long *e* sound spelled *ee*.

_____ _____ _____

Write the Spelling Words with the long *e* sound spelled *ea*.

_____ _____

_____ _____

Write the two Spelling Words you have not written.

_____ _____

Copyright © Houghton Mifflin Company. All rights reserved.

Name _____

Spelling Spree

**Rhyming Clues Write a Spelling Word
for each clue.**

Spelling Words

1. clean
2. keep
3. please
4. feel
5. we
6. be
7. eat
8. tree
9. mean
10. read
11. the*
12. people*

1. It begins with the letter **e**.

   It rhymes with **feet**. _____

2. It begins with the letters **tr**.

   It rhymes with **me**. _____

3. It begins with the letter **w**.

   It rhymes with **he**. _____

4. It begins with the letter **r**.

   It rhymes with **feed**. _____

5. It begins with the letter **b**.

   It rhymes with **see**. _____

6. It begins with the letters **cl**.

   It rhymes with **bean**. _____

7. It begins with the letter **k**.

   It rhymes with **deep**. _____

8. It begins with the letter **m**.

   It rhymes with **seen**. _____

Copyright © Houghton Mifflin Company. All rights reserved.

Name _____

Proofreading and Writing

Proofreading Circle four Spelling Words that are
spelled wrong. Then write each word correctly.

Spelling Words

1. clean
2. keep
3. please
4. feel
5. we
6. be
7. eat
8. tree
9. mean
10. read
11. the*
12. people*

New Artist in Town

Many peaple came to see th

paintings of Jamaica Louise James

yesterday. She paints the things around

her. She paints her family, houses, cats,

and dogs. One special painting is a

picture of a tree. Her paintings make us

all feal happy. Pleese don't miss her

wonderful show of paintings! The show

will be open for one more day.

1. _____ 3. _____

2. _____ 4. _____

Write a Review On a separate sheet of paper, write about
a painting you have seen. Tell what you like about the
painting. Use Spelling Words from the list.

Copyright © Houghton Mifflin Company. All rights reserved.

Name _____

Where to Find It

Word Bank

lap	laugh	drove	dream
drip	lamb	late	drum
law	dry	dress	land

**Look at the dictionary guide words below. Write each
word from the box on the correct dictionary page.**

draw / drive

_____

_____

_____

drop / duck

_____

_____

_____

lake / large

_____

_____

_____

last / lazy

_____

_____

_____

Copyright © Houghton Mifflin Company. All rights reserved.

Name _____

Which Word?

Choose the best word for each sentence and write it on the line.

1. Jamaica often plays with

   other _____.

child   children

2. One _____ gave her a
   flower.

child   children

3. Jamaica painted the _____
   with the green hat.

woman   women

4. The four _____ in the subway
   liked her paintings.

man   men

5. One _____ said the paintings
   made her feel happy.

woman   women

6. A _____ who was an artist
   looked at the paintings.

man   men

7. One _____ gave Jamaica
   a big hug.

woman   women

8. The _____ at Jamaica's school
   went to see her paintings.

child   children

Copyright © Houghton Mifflin Company. All rights reserved.

Name _____

One or More Than One

Write the word that goes with each drawing.

Word Bank

men	mice	woman	mouse
teeth	man	tooth	women

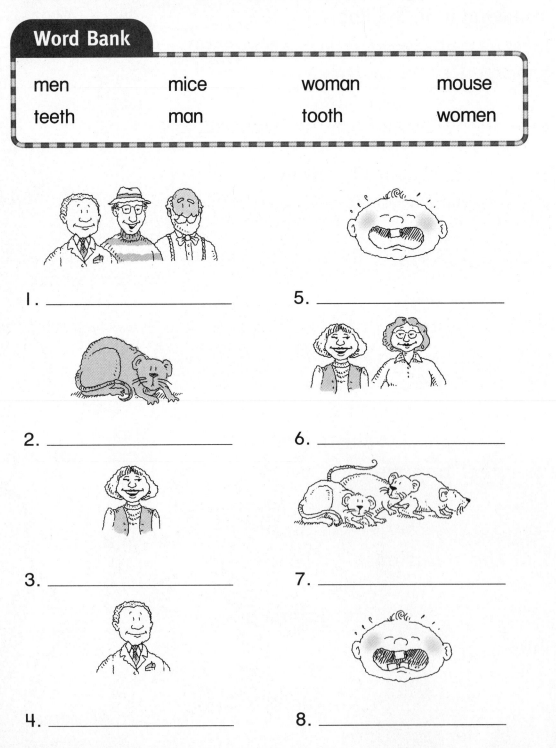

1. _____

2. _____

3. _____

4. _____

5. _____

6. _____

7. _____

8. _____

Copyright © Houghton Mifflin Company. All rights reserved.

Name _____

What's the Plural?

Circle the five words that are not correct. Then write each word correctly.

March 3, 2001

> Today I saw three womans wearing big hats. The hats had bright yellow flowers on them. I saw two childs playing in the park. They had pet mouses that crawled up their arms. I wonder if a mouse has sharp tooths. Then I saw four mans carrying a piano. Their faces were red.

1. _____

2. _____

3. _____

4. _____

5. _____

Copyright © Houghton Mifflin Company. All rights reserved.

Name _____

Get Ready to Write Your Ad

Use this form to help you write your ad. Remember that you are trying to convince someone to buy your product. Think about who might buy it and what you could say to convince them to buy it.

James Advertising Agency

Name of what I'm going to sell: _____

Who will buy it? _____

Tell about the person who will buy it. _____

_____

_____

Tell why your product is special. _____

_____

Name two reasons why someone should buy it.

_____

_____

Copyright © Houghton Mifflin Company. All rights reserved.

Name _____

Who Will Use It?

Here are three items for sale. On each line, write who
might buy the item. Then read what the ad might say.
Circle the best phrase for each ad.

Who will use it?

Easy to Use!

Dries in 2 Days

Child-proof Bottle

_____

Who will use it?

Smells Like Bubble Gum!

Makes Shaving Easy!

Great for Art Projects!

_____

Who will use it?

Fresh Smell of Hay!

Smell Like a Rose Garden!

Attracts Bees Like Daisies Do!

_____

Copyright © Houghton Mifflin Company. All rights reserved.

Name _____

Writing a Personal Response

Use the test-taking strategies and tips you have learned to help you answer questions that ask what you think about something. Then read your answer and see how you may make it better. This practice will help you when you take this kind of test.

Choose one idea to write about. Write at least one paragraph about your topic.

a. How do you know that the boy and his grandmother enjoy being together in the story *Chinatown*? With which family member do you like spending time? What do you do together?

b. Why do you think the New Year's celebration is important to the boy and his grandmother? Tell about a celebration that is important to you. What is the celebration? Why is it important to you?

_____

_____

_____

_____

Copyright © Houghton Mifflin Company. All rights reserved.

Name _____

Writing a Personal Response

continued

Read your answer. Check to be sure that it

- sticks to the topic
- is well organized
- has details that support your answer
- has describing and exact words
- has few mistakes in capitalization, punctuation, grammar, or spelling

Now pick one way you can make your answer better.

Make your changes below.

_____

_____

_____

_____

_____

_____

_____

Copyright © Houghton Mifflin Company. All rights reserved.

Name _____

Spelling Review

Write Spelling Words to answer the questions.

Copyright © Houghton Mifflin Company. All rights reserved.

1–8. Which words are spelled with **th**, **wh**, **sh**, or **ch**?

1. _____   5. _____

2. _____   6. _____

3. _____   7. _____

4. _____   8. _____

9–17. Which words that you haven't written have the long **a** or long **e** sound?

9. _____   14. _____

10. _____   15. _____

11. _____   16. _____

12. _____   17. _____

13. _____

18–20. Which words have the vowel sound in **cow**?

18. _____   19. _____   20. _____

Spelling Words

1. tray
2. when
3. teeth
4. than
5. be
6. eat
7. sheep
8. play
9. frown
10. sail
11. chase
12. teach
13. please
14. train
15. wash
16. which
17. found
18. we
19. tree
20. mouse

Name _____

Around Town:
Neighborhood and
Community: Theme 3
Wrap-Up

Spelling Review

Spelling Spree

Hidden Words Circle the Spelling Word hidden in each group of letters below. Write the word on the line.

1. lpmouseto _____

2. qtreemba _____

3. arlfrownp _____

4. vgiwhich _____

5. fsheepmse _____

Spelling Words

1. frown
2. teach
3. tree
4. sheep
5. which
6. mouse
7. we
8. play
9. sail
10. found

Rhyming Clues Write a Spelling Word for each clue.

6. It rhymes with **round**.
   It begins like **fan**. _____

7. It rhymes with **beach**.
   It begins like **table**. _____

8. It rhymes with **gray**.
   It begins like **plate**. _____

9. It rhymes with **be**.
   It begins like **worm**. _____

10. It rhymes with **mail**.
    It begins like **sun**. _____

Copyright © Houghton Mifflin Company. All rights reserved.

Name _____

Around Town:
Neighborhood and
Community: Theme 3
Wrap-Up

Spelling Review

Proofreading and Writing

Proofreading Circle four Spelling Words that are wrong. Then write each word correctly.

Spelling Words

Come to a block party! It will bea this Friday. Come enjoy good things to eet. Bring the whole family, plese!

The party starts at five P.M. It will end wen you want to go home!

Spelling Words
1. chase
2. when
3. train
4. than
5. please
6. teeth
7. be
8. wash
9. tray
10. eat

1. _____   3. _____

2. _____   4. _____

A Party Plan Write Spelling Words to complete this plan.

Dad, take the early 5._____ home. Mom,

6._____ the vegetables for the party and put them

on a 7._____. Maya, don't let the dog

8._____ the cat! T.J., brush your 9._____.

We'll have more fun 10._____ we've ever had!

Write a Diary Entry Write a diary entry about the block party. Use another sheet of paper. Use the Spelling Review Words.

Copyright © Houghton Mifflin Company. All rights reserved.

My Handbook

Copyright © Houghton Mifflin Company. All rights reserved.

Contents

Copyright © Houghton Mifflin Company. All rights reserved.

Trace and write the letters.

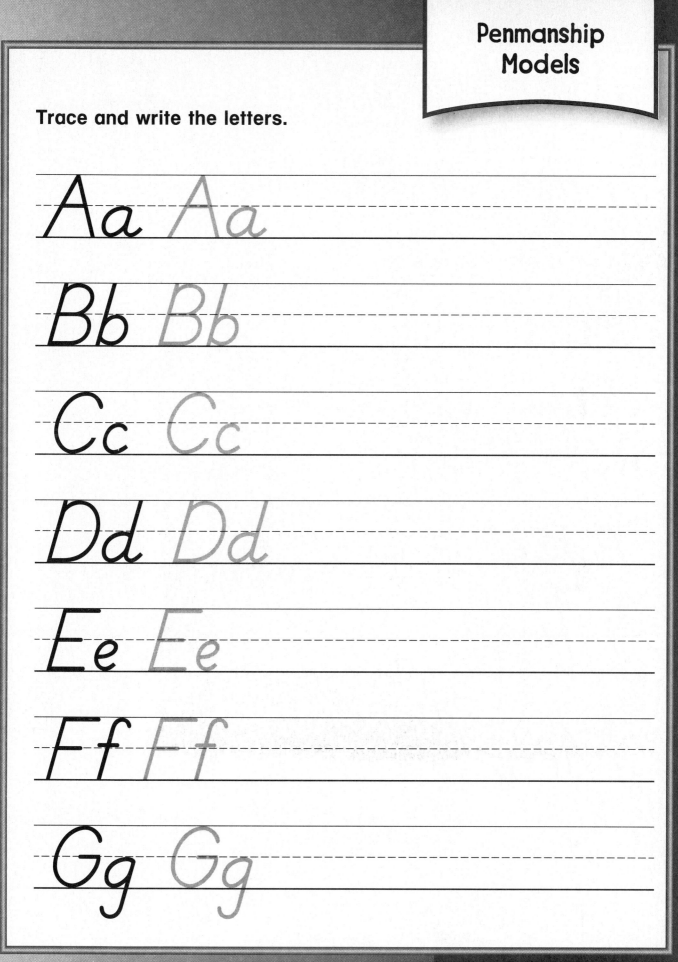

Aa Aa

Bb Bb

Cc Cc

Dd Dd

Ee Ee

Ff Ff

Gg Gg

Copyright © Houghton Mifflin Company. All rights reserved.

Trace and write the letters.

Hh Hh

Ii Ii

Jj Jj

Kk Kk

Ll Ll

Mm Mm

222   **My Handbook**

Copyright © Houghton Mifflin Company. All rights reserved.

Trace and write the letters.

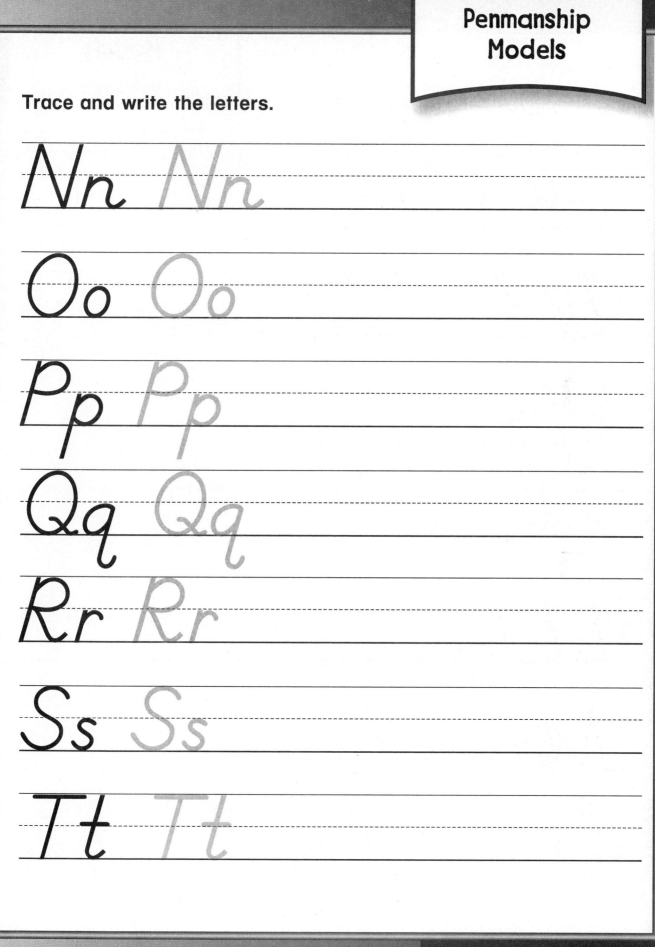

Nn Nn

Oo Oo

Pp Pp

Qq Qq

Rr Rr

Ss Ss

Tt Tt

Copyright © Houghton Mifflin Company. All rights reserved.

Trace and write the letters.

Uu *Uu*

Vv *Vv*

Ww *Ww*

Xx *Xx*

Yy *Yy*

Zz *Zz*

Copyright © Houghton Mifflin Company. All rights reserved.

Trace and write the letters.

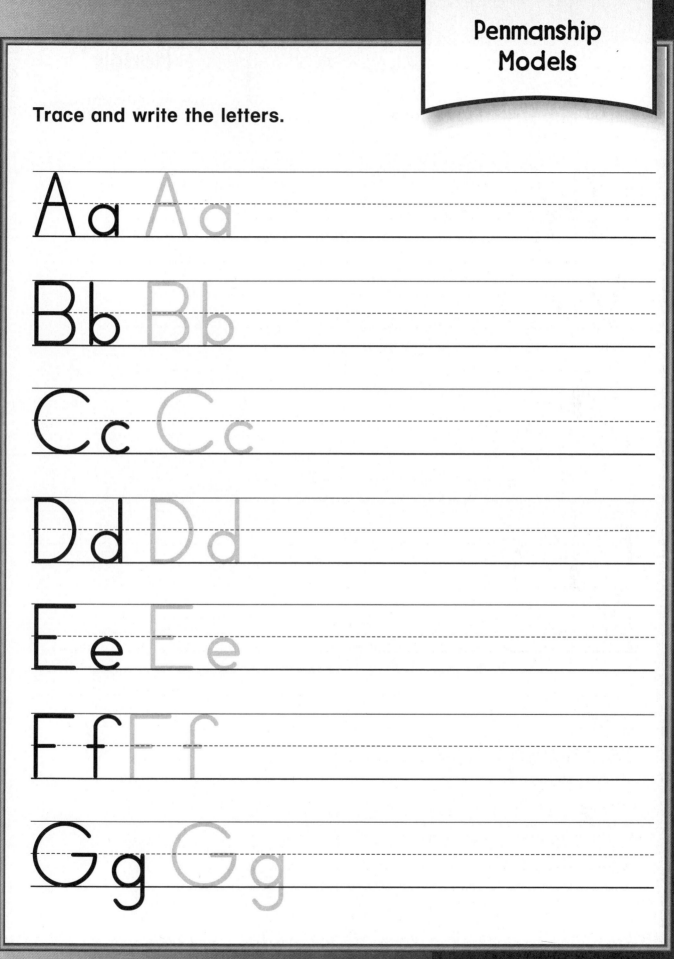

Copyright © Houghton Mifflin Company. All rights reserved.

Trace and write the letters.

Hh Hh

Ii Ii

Jj Jj

Kk Kk

Ll Ll

Mm Mm

Copyright © Houghton Mifflin Company. All rights reserved.

Trace and write the letters.

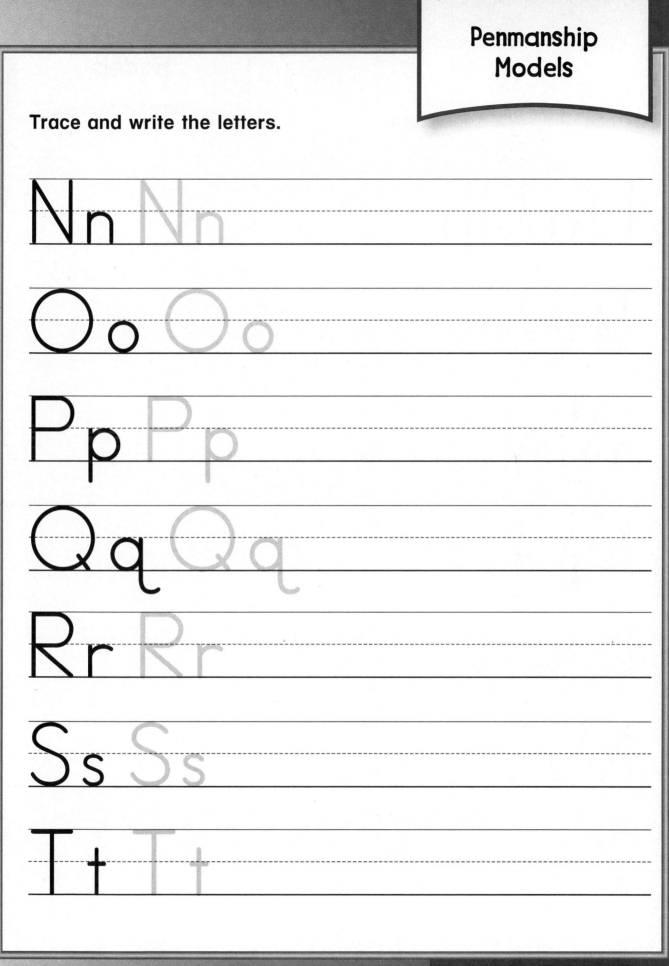

Copyright © Houghton Mifflin Company. All rights reserved.

Trace and write the letters.

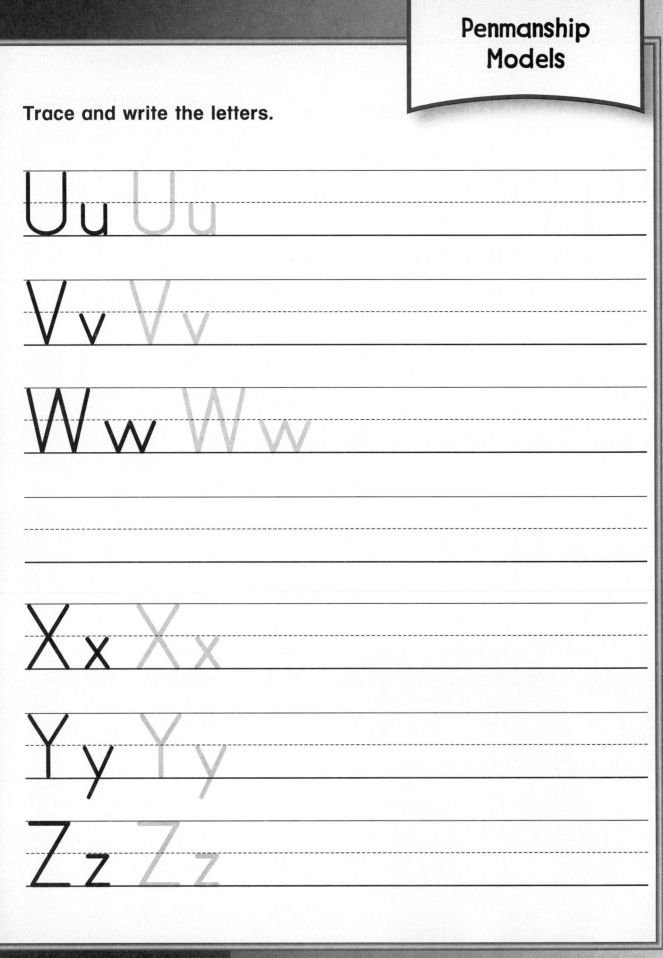

Copyright © Houghton Mifflin Company. All rights reserved.

How to Study a Word

1. LOOK at the word.
► What does the word mean?
► What letters are in the word?
► Name and touch each letter.

2. SAY the word.
► Listen for the consonant sounds.
► Listen for the vowel sounds.

3. THINK about the word.
► How is each sound spelled?
► Close your eyes and picture the word.
► What other words have the same spelling patterns?

4. WRITE the word.
► Think about the sounds and the letters.
► Form the letters correctly.

5. CHECK the spelling.
► Did you spell the word the same way it is spelled in your word list?
► Write the word again if you did not spell it correctly.

Copyright © Houghton Mifflin Company. All rights reserved.

A
about
again
a lot
always
am
and
any
are
around
as

B
back
because
been
before

C
cannot
caught
come
coming
could

D
do
does
done
down

E
enough

F
family
first
for
found
friend
from

G
getting
girl
goes
going

H
has
have
heard
her
here
his
how

I
I'd
if
I'll
I'm
into

it
it's

K
knew
know

L
letter
little

M
many
more
my
myself

N
name
never
new
now

O
of
off
on
once
one
other
our
outside

P
people
pretty

R
really
right

S
said
school
some
something
started
stopped

T
that's
the
their
there
they
thought
through
time
to
today
too

tried
two

V
very

W
want
was
went
were
what
when
where
who
will
would
write

Y
you
your

Copyright © Houghton Mifflin Company. All rights reserved.

Silly Stories:

Reading-Writing Workshop

Look carefully at how these words are spelled.

Dragon Gets By

The Short *a* and Short *i* Sounds

short **a** sound ➤ **am**

　　　　　　　　 b**a**g

short **i** sound ➤ **is**

　　　　　　　　 d**i**g

Spelling Words

1. the	7. it
2. will	8. they
3. have	9. as
4. was	10. my
5. you	11. off
6. said	12. any

Spelling Words

1. bag	7. ran
2. win	8. if
3. is	9. dig
4. am	10. sat
5. his	11. was
6. has	12. I

Challenge Words

1. because
2. family

Challenge Words

1. scratch
2. picnic

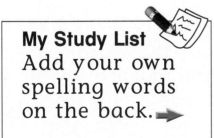

My Study List
Add your own spelling words on the back. ➤

My Study List
Add your own spelling words on the back. ➤

Copyright © Houghton Mifflin Company. All rights reserved.

Name_____

My Study List

1. _____

2. _____

3. _____

4. _____

5. _____

6. _____

7. _____

8. _____

9. _____

10. _____

Review Words

1. big
2. an

How to Study a Word

Look at the word.
Say the word.
Think about the word.
Write the word.
Check the spelling.

Take-Home Word List

Name_____

My Study List

1. _____

2. _____

3. _____

4. _____

5. _____

6. _____

7. _____

8. _____

9. _____

10. _____

How to Study a Word

Look at the word.
Say the word.
Think about the word.
Write the word.
Check the spelling.

232

Copyright © Houghton Mifflin Company. All rights reserved.

Mrs. Brown Went to Town

Vowel-Consonant-*e* Spellings

long **a** sound ➡ **late**

long **i** sound ➡ **bite**

Spelling Words

1. bite	7. fine
2. late	8. same
3. size	9. hide
4. made	10. line
5. side	11. give
6. ate	12. have

Challenge Words

1. shake
2. write

Julius

The Short *e, o,* and *u* Sounds

short **e** sound ➡ wet, leg

short **o** sound ➡ job, mop

short **u** sound ➡ nut, fun

Spelling Words

1. fox	7. went
2. wet	8. mop
3. nut	9. hug
4. job	10. from
5. leg	11. any
6. fun	12. of

Challenge Words

1. block
2. every

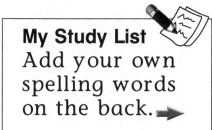

My Study List
Add your own
spelling words
on the back. ➡

My Study List
Add your own
spelling words
on the back. ➡

Copyright © Houghton Mifflin Company. All rights reserved.

Take-Home Word List

Name_____

My Study List

1. _____
2. _____
3. _____
4. _____
5. _____
6. _____
7. _____
8. _____
9. _____
10. _____

Review Words

1. red
2. up

How to Study a Word

Look at the word.
Say the word.
Think about the word.
Write the word.
Check the spelling.

234

Take-Home Word List

Name_____

My Study List

1. _____
2. _____
3. _____
4. _____
5. _____
6. _____
7. _____
8. _____
9. _____
10. _____

Review Words

1. gate
2. bike

How to Study a Word

Look at the word.
Say the word.
Think about the word.
Write the word.
Check the spelling.

234

Copyright © Houghton Mifflin Company. All rights reserved.

Henry and Mudge and the Starry Night

More Vowel-Consonant-*e* Spellings

long **e** → th**ese**

long **o** → b**one**

long **u** → **use**

Spelling Words

1. bone
2. robe
3. use
4. these
5. rope
6. note
7. cute
8. close
9. hope
10. those
11. one
12. goes

Challenge Words

1. drove
2. mule

Silly Stories Spelling Review

Spelling Words

1. am
2. dig
3. fox
4. nut
5. leg
6. hide
7. late
8. ran
9. job
10. fun
11. wet
12. bite
13. made
14. ate
15. sat
16. mop
17. hug
18. went
19. size
20. his

Challenge Words

1. scratch
2. block
3. every
4. shake
5. write

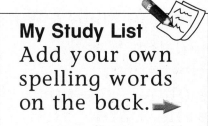

My Study List
Add your own spelling words on the back. ➡

My Study List
Add your own spelling words on the back. ➡

Copyright © Houghton Mifflin Company. All rights reserved.

Take-Home Word List

Name_____

My Study List

1. _____
2. _____
3. _____
4. _____
5. _____
6. _____
7. _____
8. _____
9. _____
10. _____

How to Study a Word

Look at the word.
Say the word.
Think about the word.
Write the word.
Check the spelling.

236

Take-Home Word List

Name_____

My Study List

1. _____
2. _____
3. _____
4. _____
5. _____
6. _____
7. _____
8. _____
9. _____
10. _____

Review Words

1. home
2. nose

How to Study a Word

Look at the word.
Say the word.
Think about the word.
Write the word.
Check the spelling.

236

Copyright © Houghton Mifflin Company. All rights reserved.

Exploring Parks with
Ranger Dockett

Words with Consonant Clusters
trip, **sw**im, **st**ep, **cl**ub,
ne**xt, br**ave, **gl**ad

Spelling Words

1. trip	6. stone
2. swim	7. next
3. step	8. brave
4. nest	9. glad
5. club	10. lost

Challenge Words

1. space
2. storm

Nature Walk
Reading-Writing Workshop

Look carefully at how these words are spelled.

Spelling Words

1. on	7. come
2. am	8. want
3. if	9. does
4. from	10. goes
5. his	11. their
6. her	12. there

Challenge Words

1. really
2. caught

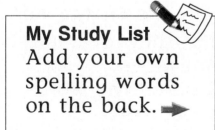

My Study List
Add your own
spelling words
on the back. ➡

My Study List
Add your own
spelling words
on the back. ➡

Copyright © Houghton Mifflin Company. All rights reserved.

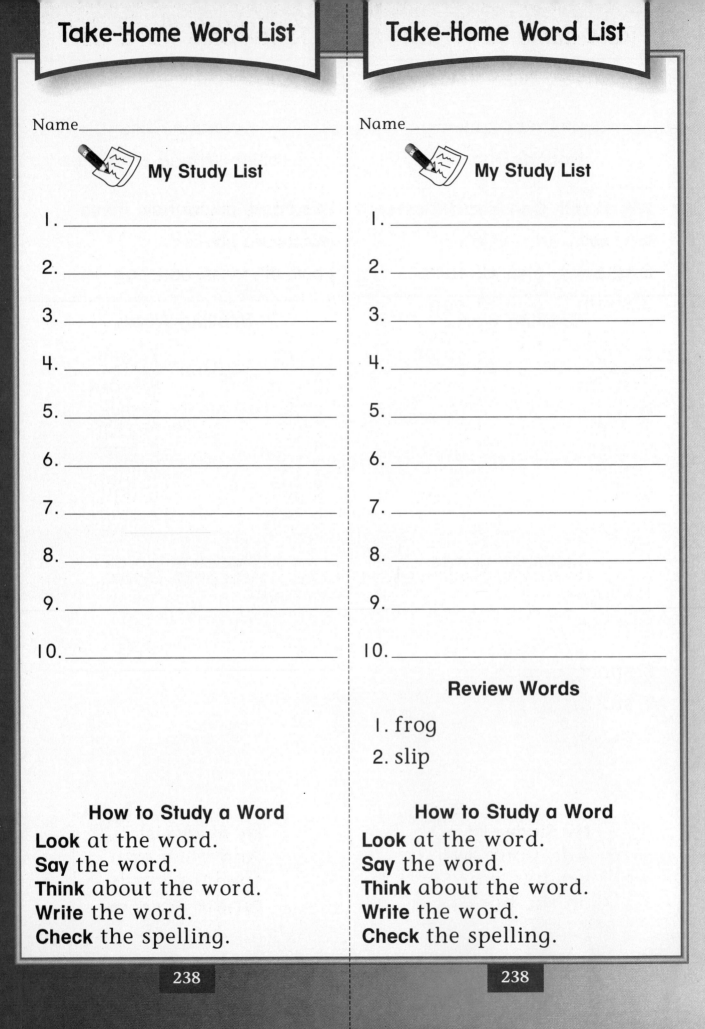

Take-Home Word List

Name_____

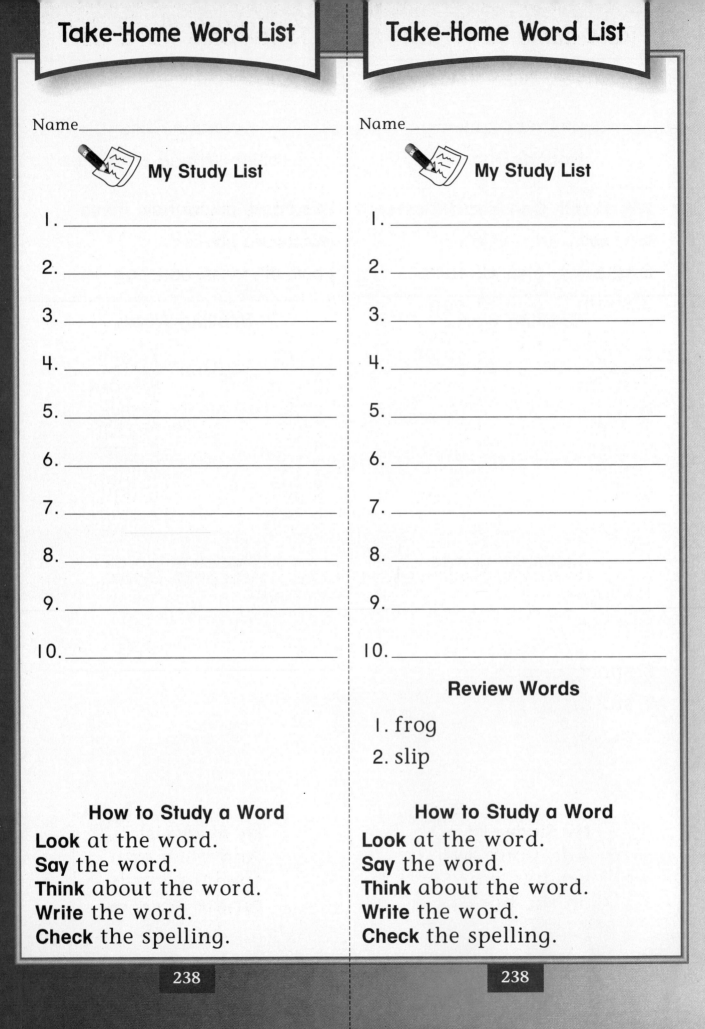 **My Study List**

1._____

2._____

3._____

4._____

5._____

6._____

7._____

8._____

9._____

10._____

How to Study a Word
Look at the word.
Say the word.
Think about the word.
Write the word.
Check the spelling.

Take-Home Word List

Name_____

My Study List

1._____

2._____

3._____

4._____

5._____

6._____

7._____

8._____

9._____

10._____

Review Words

1. frog
2. slip

How to Study a Word
Look at the word.
Say the word.
Think about the word.
Write the word.
Check the spelling.

Copyright © Houghton Mifflin Company. All rights reserved.

Nature Walk
Spelling Review

Spelling Words

1. these
2. use
3. swim
4. glad
5. club
6. all
7. bone
8. cute
9. next
10. brave
11. add
12. mess
13. egg
14. hope
15. trip
16. stone
17. lost
18. off
19. grass
20. hill

Challenge Words

1. drove
2. mule
3. space
4. storm
5. across

My Study List
Add your own spelling words on the back. ➡

Around the Pond:
Who's Been Here?

Words with Double Consonants
bell, off, mess, add, egg

Spelling Words

1. bell
2. off
3. all
4. mess
5. add
6. hill
7. well
8. egg
9. will
10. grass

Challenge Words

1. across
2. skill

My Study List
Add your own spelling words on the back. ➡

Copyright © Houghton Mifflin Company. All rights reserved.

Take-Home Word List

Name_____

My Study List

1. _____
2. _____
3. _____
4. _____
5. _____
6. _____
7. _____
8. _____
9. _____
10. _____

Review Words

1. shell
2. kiss

How to Study a Word

Look at the word.
Say the word.
Think about the word.
Write the word.
Check the spelling.

Take-Home Word List

Name_____

My Study List

1. _____
2. _____
3. _____
4. _____
5. _____
6. _____
7. _____
8. _____
9. _____
10. _____

How to Study a Word

Look at the word.
Say the word.
Think about the word.
Write the word.
Check the spelling.

Copyright © Houghton Mifflin Company. All rights reserved.

Around Town:

Neighborhood and Community
Reading-Writing Workshop

Look carefully at how these words are spelled.

Chinatown

Words Spelled with _th, wh, sh,_ or _ch_

the **th** sound → **th**en, tee**th**

the **wh** sound → **wh**en

the **sh** sound → **sh**eep, di**sh**

the **ch** sound → **ch**ase, tea**ch**

Spelling Words

1. write
2. of
3. do
4. to
5. time
6. went
7. myself
8. what
9. name
10. too
11. little
12. been

Spelling Words

1. when
2. sheep
3. both
4. then
5. chase
6. teeth
7. teach
8. dish
9. which
10. than
11. wash
12. catch

Challenge Words

1. right
2. thought

Challenge Words

1. lunch
2. whistle

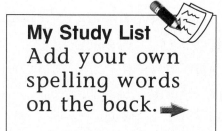

My Study List
Add your own spelling words on the back. ➡

My Study List
Add your own spelling words on the back. ➡

Copyright © Houghton Mifflin Company. All rights reserved.

Take-Home Word List

Take-Home Word List

Name_____

My Study List

1. _____
2. _____
3. _____
4. _____
5. _____
6. _____
7. _____
8. _____
9. _____
10. _____

Review Words

1. she
2. bath

How to Study a Word

Look at the word.
Say the word.
Think about the word.
Write the word.
Check the spelling.

242

Name_____

My Study List

1. _____
2. _____
3. _____
4. _____
5. _____
6. _____
7. _____
8. _____
9. _____
10. _____

How to Study a Word

Look at the word.
Say the word.
Think about the word.
Write the word.
Check the spelling.

242

Copyright © Houghton Mifflin Company. All rights reserved.

Take-Home Word List

Big Bushy Mustache

The Vowel Sound in *cow*

ow → town

ou → house

Spelling Words

1. town
2. house
3. sour
4. frown
5. cow
6. clown
7. found
8. how
9. mouse
10. brown
11. could
12. should

Challenge Words

1. around
2. towel

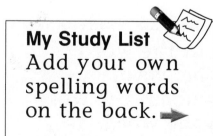

My Study List
Add your own spelling words on the back. →

Take-Home Word List

A Trip to the Firehouse

More Long *a* Spellings

long **a** sound → tr**ay**, tr**ai**n

Spelling Words

1. train
2. tray
3. mail
4. play
5. trail
6. pay
7. sail
8. hay
9. nail
10. rain
11. they
12. great

Challenge Words

1. snail
2. subway

My Study List
Add your own spelling words on the back. →

Copyright © Houghton Mifflin Company. All rights reserved.

Take-Home Word List

Take-Home Word List

Name_____

My Study List

1. _____
2. _____
3. _____
4. _____
5. _____
6. _____
7. _____
8. _____
9. _____
10. _____

Review Words

1. stay
2. day

How to Study a Word

Look at the word.
Say the word.
Think about the word.
Write the word.
Check the spelling.

Name_____

My Study List

1. _____
2. _____
3. _____
4. _____
5. _____
6. _____
7. _____
8. _____
9. _____
10. _____

Review Words

1. out
2. now

How to Study a Word

Look at the word.
Say the word.
Think about the word.
Write the word.
Check the spelling.

Copyright © Houghton Mifflin Company. All rights reserved.

Around Town:
Neighborhood and Community
Spelling Review

Spelling Words

1. which	11. sail
2. teach	12. found
3. wash	13. be
4. tray	14. tree
5. frown	15. chase
6. we	16. than
7. eat	17. play
8. when	18. train
9. teeth	19. mouse
10. sheep	20. please

Challenge Words

1. lunch
2. whistle
3. snail
4. around
5. steep

My Study List
Add your own spelling words on the back. ➡

Jamaica Louise James

More Long *e* Spellings
long **e** sound ➡ w**e**
k**ee**p
cl**ea**n

Spelling Words

1. clean	7. eat
2. keep	8. tree
3. please	9. mean
4. feel	10. read
5. we	11. the
6. be	12. people

Challenge Words

1. stream
2. steep

My Study List
Add your own spelling words on the back. ➡

Copyright © Houghton Mifflin Company. All rights reserved.

Name_____

My Study List

1. _____
2. _____
3. _____
4. _____
5. _____
6. _____
7. _____
8. _____
9. _____
10. _____

Review Words

1. he
2. see

How to Study a Word

Look at the word.
Say the word.
Think about the word.
Write the word.
Check the spelling.

246

Name_____

My Study List

1. _____
2. _____
3. _____
4. _____
5. _____
6. _____
7. _____
8. _____
9. _____
10. _____

How to Study a Word

Look at the word.
Say the word.
Think about the word.
Write the word.
Check the spelling.

246

Copyright © Houghton Mifflin Company. All rights reserved.

Read each question. Check your paper for each kind of mistake. Correct any mistakes you find.

☐ Did I begin each sentence with a capital letter?

☐ Did I use the correct end mark?

☐ Did I spell each word correctly?

☐ Did I indent each paragraph?

Proofreading Marks		
∧	Add one or more words.	want to I see the play. ∧
—	Take out one or more words. Change the spelling.	The boat ~~did~~ moved slowly. filled The cloud ~~filed~~ the sky.
/	Make a capital letter a small letter.	The A̷nimals hid from the storm.
☰	Make a small letter a capital letter.	There are thirty days in a̲p̲ril.

Copyright © Houghton Mifflin Company. All rights reserved.

Copyright © Houghton Mifflin Company. All rights reserved.

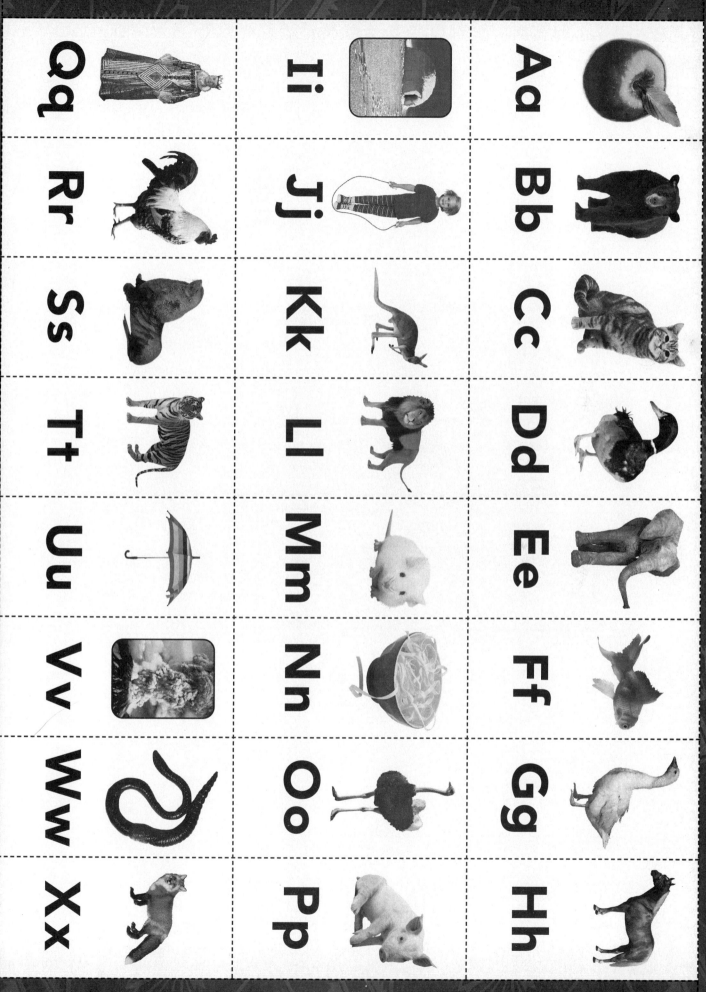

Qq | Ii | Aa
Rr | Jj | Bb
Ss | Kk | Cc
Tt | Ll | Dd
Uu | Mm | Ee
Vv | Nn | Ff
Ww | Oo | Gg
Xx | Pp | Hh

Copyright © Houghton Mifflin Company. All rights reserved.

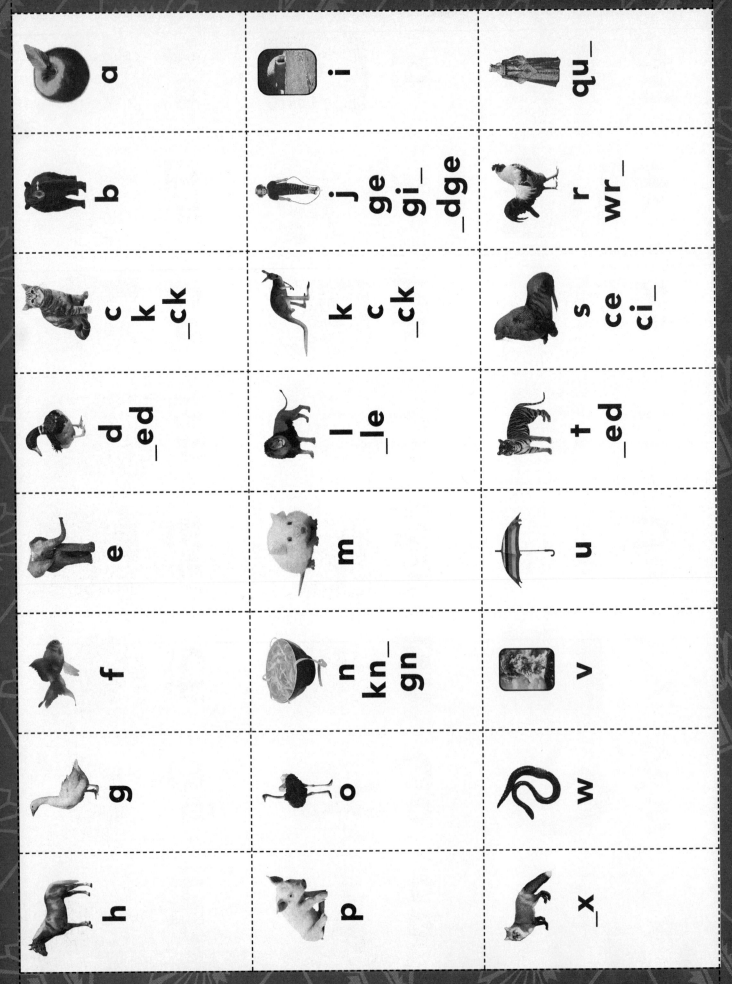

a	i	qu_
b	j ge gi_ _dge	r wr_
c k _ck	k c _ck	s ce ci_
d _ed	l _le	t _ed
e	m	u
f	n kn_ _gn	v
g	o	w
h	p	x _

Copyright © Houghton Mifflin Company. All rights reserved.

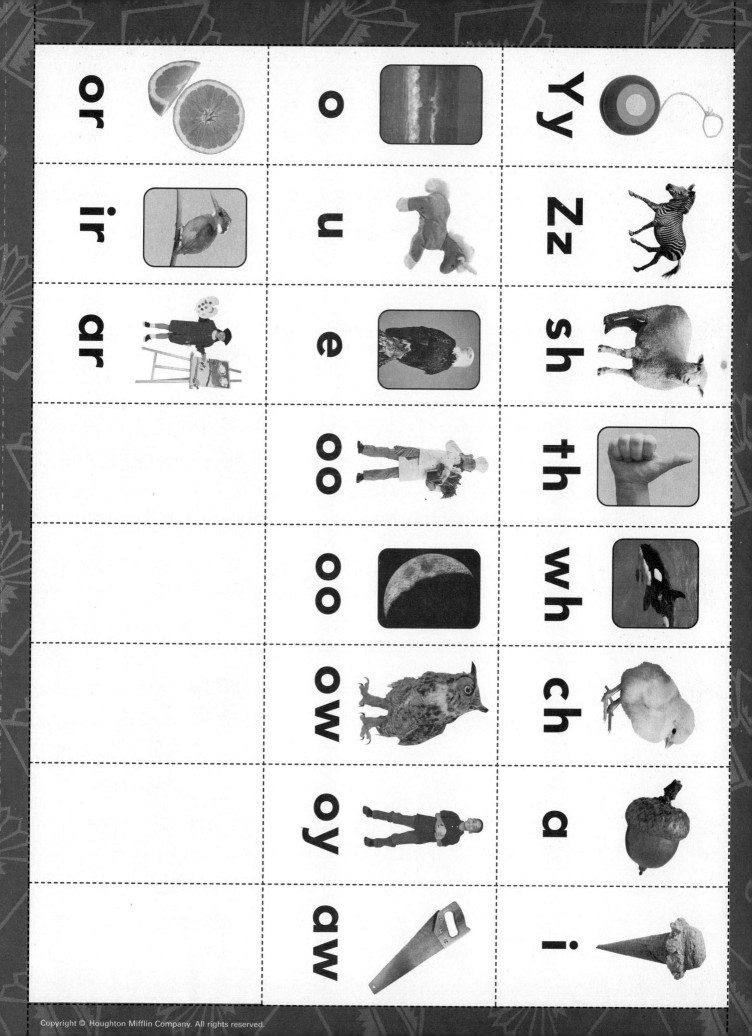

or	**o**	**Yy**
ir	**u**	**Zz**
ar	**e**	**sh**
	oo	**th**
	oo	**wh**
	ow	**ch**
	oy	**a**
	aw	**i**

Copyright © Houghton Mifflin Company. All rights reserved.

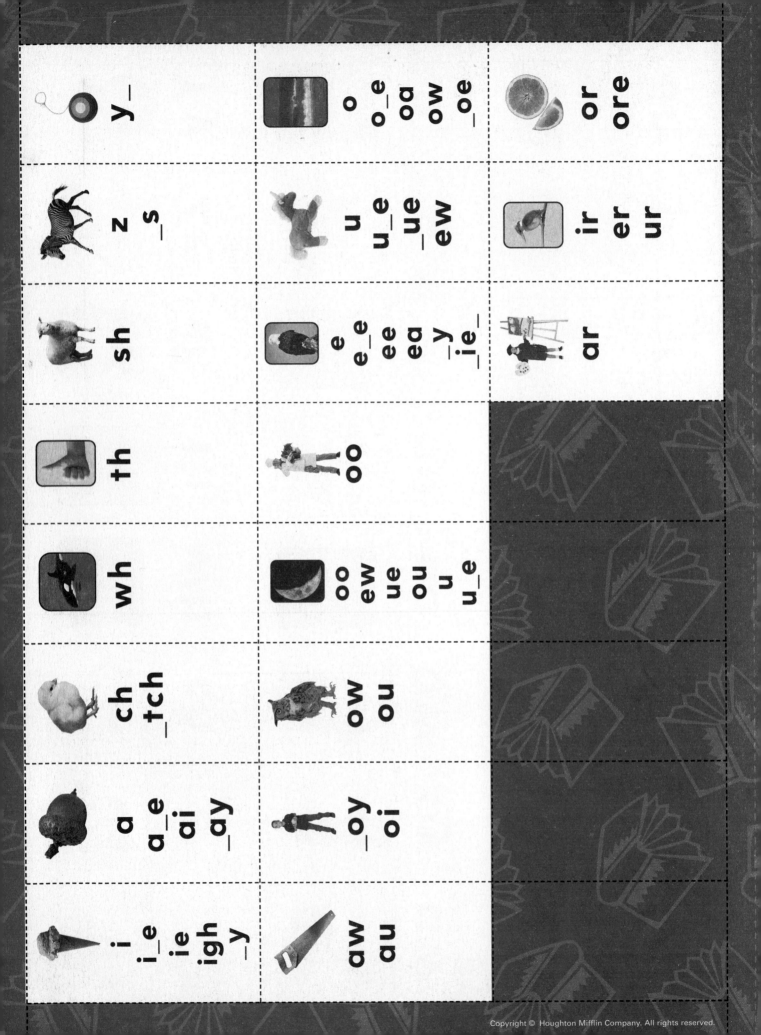 y_	o / o_e / oa / ow / _oe	or / ore
z / _s	u / u_e / _ue / ew	ir / er / ur
sh	e / e_e / ee / ea / _y / ie_	ar
th	oo	
wh	oo / ew / ue / ou / u / u_e	
ch / _tch	ow / ou	
a / a_e / ai / _ay	_oy / oi	
i / i_e / ie / igh / _y	aw / au	

Copyright © Houghton Mifflin Company. All rights reserved.